Live to Forgive

Moving Forward When Those
We Love Hurt Us

Jason Romano

with Stephen Copeland
Foreword by Darryl Strawberry

CORE.

Matt 28:20

Live to Forgive

Published by The Core Media Group, Inc., P.O. Box 2037, Indian Trail, NC 28079.

Cover & Interior Design: Nadia Guy

Printed in the Pereira, Colombia.

To George Romano, my grandfather who we called "Pa."

I am who I am because of you.

I pray your legacy continues to live on through your grandchildren—Chris, Damian, and myself—and through your son, Joe Romano, my dad.

Praise for *Live to Forgive*

"I worked with Jason at ESPN but didn't know that he had a gift for preaching until I happened to be at Hillside Community Church in Bristol, Connecticut, when he was filling in for his pastor and delivering a sermon. His sermon opened up the gate for the two of us to talk about matters of faith, and I'm confident that his book *Live to Forgive* will open up the gate to a serious nationwide discussion about forgiveness. I'm thankful for Jason's testimony and his commitment to help others with their deepest pains and needs."

Darren Woodson, Dallas Cowboys Safety,
Three-Time Super Bowl Champion

"In a world that tells us it's best to mask our pain, keep our brokenness hidden and simply 'move on' amidst the chaos of unresolved tension and wounds, Jason's words are raw, vulnerable, and refreshing. Forgiveness is the key to unlocking true freedom, but the process of forgiving those who have hurt us often invites us into painful territory. It's gut-wrenching...but it's glory. Jason has done an outstanding job of inviting the reader into the hardest parts of his life and, in turn, out of the valleys of their own."

Mo Isom, *New York Times* Bestselling Author of *Wreck My Life*

"As a songwriter, my goal is to say something fresh in each song—to tell a story in some way. Jason's book *Live to Forgive* is a fresh approach to forgiveness, told through the power of story."

Mac Powell, Singer, Songwriter, and Musician;
Third Day Frontman

"I used to call Jason Romano 'the nicest guy at ESPN.' It was the truth. I loved not only working with Jason for eight years at ESPN-NFL but also our private conversations about life and spirituality. Like Jason, I have had to cope with loss and trauma in my life and find a way to forgive. This is a much-needed book in our culture and will help to set a lot of people free."

Trent Dilfer, Former ESPN-NFL Analyst,
Super Bowl XXXV Champion

"In a world that emphasizes power and control, *Live to Forgive* is a breath of fresh air. My friend Jason Romano compels us to see that real strength and true freedom are experienced when we forgive those who hurt us the most."

Caleb Kaltenbach,
Author of *Messy Grace* and *God of Tomorrow*

"Jason Romano and I are one in the same. We are both followers of Christ, people who are ministry-focused, and former ESPN employees. As Jason has followed the Lord, I have seen him remain true to his convictions and take more risks in his life for the glory of God. This book is a culmination of his spiritual journey, as God has challenged him more and more to share his story with others in order to bring hope and joy into brokenness."

Chris Broussard, Fox Sports Analyst

"The more I've gotten to know Jason Romano the more I have admired him and his leadership. After all, how many would leave a dream job at ESPN to pursue their calling in ministry? And the fact that he would have the courage to write this very painful and personal story of forgiveness to bring true healing into the world says everything about him and this amazing book. Read it today!"

Jon Gordon,
Bestselling Author of *The Energy Bus* and *The Carpenter*

"Jason Romano is a powerful storyteller and compelling writer. Readers will appreciate his honesty, compassion and the care in which he handles the difficult subject of forgiveness."

Jemele Hill, ESPN SportsCenter Host

"I have always admired Jason's ability to connect two things that I am passionate about: faith and sports. He is a natural leader who effectively uses his platform to bring hope into people's lives. In *Live to Forgive*, Jason's story is an invitation to you for moving forward in your own journey of forgiveness. There is hope on the other side of bitterness, so let Jason be your guide as you move towards freedom."

Brad Lomenick,
Author of *The Catalyst Leader* and *H3 Leadership*

"In his willingness to open up about his painful past, Jason cuts to the heart of one of our most basic human needs. Jason's vulnerable yet practical style takes us on a journey to find the peace that only comes with forgiveness."

Amy Lawrence, CBS Sports Radio Host

"Jason Romano gave me my first shot to be on television and has helped me to grow in my career. Even more, I have had very deep, long conversations with him about life, faith, and family. I have always appreciated his wisdom and insight. After reading *Live to Forgive*, I could suddenly see where his wisdom came from: the difficulties in his life that he has endured and the pain that he has surrendered to God to transform. This book will help you to do the same and live a meaningful life that is rooted in God's love and grace."

Ryan Clark, ESPN-NFL Analyst,
Super Bowl XLIII Champion

"My friend Jason Romano's story of pain and forgiveness resonates deeply with me, as I know it will with countless readers. He shares his heartbreaking, gut-wrenching experiences with complete transparency and raw emotion, making his message of love and redemption even more powerful. If you've met Jason personally, you know He loves Jesus. His passion for the Lord is unmistakable. And when you hear about the pain of his past, you understand exactly where this passion comes from. Jason's life was radically changed by love and forgiveness, and I am absolutely thrilled he is sharing his testimony with the world. This book *will* impact your life."

Kelli Masters, NFL Player Agent

"One of my passions is to bring hope to a fatherless generation—to help people rise above the challenges of not having a good father figure in their life and still make decisions that cultivate excellence and success. My dear friend, Jason Romano, took the pain in his own life—stemming from his father—and used it to strengthen his mission in the world and bring hope to others. His book is a must-read for all, as we are each challenged to make the most of the hand that we have been dealt and become who God intended us to be."

Benjamin Watson, NFL Tight End,
Author of *Under Our Skin* and *The New Dad's Playbook*

"I know of no one more decent, honest, and committed to his faith than Jason Romano, so it is no surprise he's written a book of such searing honesty and emotion. *Live to Forgive* has a message as real as the lives from which it is drawn. There are challenges and hurdles, pain and tears, and an important message seen through Jason's relationship with his father. You'll be touched, and you'll be informed. And you'll be better for reading it."

Bob Ley, ESPN Anchor

"From the moment I encountered Jason I knew he was different. His light, a direct reflection of God, is so inviting and warm that you instantly want to know more about Jason and this God he serves. I'm so grateful Jason was faithful to his calling and wrote this book. So many will be saved because of it. So many will start to see themselves as a beautiful masterpiece because of it. And that is the true miracle of it all!"

Rachel Baribeau, ESPNU SiriusXM Host

"One of my favorite things each time that I did the 'ESPN Car Wash' was spending time with one of ESPN's employees, Jason Romano. Not only did Jason and I share a love for the New York Mets, where I spent the first ten years of my career, but both of our lives have also been shaped by addiction. When I visited ESPN in 2011, I asked Jason how his father was doing, and he shared with me that his dad's alcoholism and depression was spiraling out of control. I asked Jason for his father's number and decided to give him a call. Turns out, I talked to his dad merely days before his suicide attempt. In this book, not only will you learn the process of forgiving, but you will also learn how to treat someone who is suffering from addiction or alcoholism. This is a must-read for anyone struggling with forgiveness, bitterness, or the ripple-effects of addiction."

Dwight "Doc" Gooden, Author of *Doc: A Memoir*,
Three-Time World Series champion, 1985 NL Cy Young Winner

"Jason's story means a lot to me. I, too, had a challenging relationship with my father. It took me a long time to forgive him for the abuse he caused me, and there were many days where I felt like I might not ever be able to. Forgiveness is a difficult thing. Jason does not sugarcoat the process in his book *Live to Forgive*. He challenges readers to enter into the messiness of the healing process, something that involves a lot of hard work. It was challenging, too, for me to do this—but once I allowed myself to feel, evaluate, and transform my pain, I began to step into the freedom of forgiveness."

Bart Millard, MercyMe Lead Singer,
Author of *The Hurt & The Healer*

"When I first met Jason in 2012 at ESPN, I was trying to get my life back on track. I was haunted by a past that was full of mistakes. But the thing that Jason and I talked about the most when I met him was redemption—redemption through Jesus Christ. Now I can see that Jason had a lot of experience with redemption, too—in his relationship with his father. This book will challenge you to transform your pain and make the most of your life—to experience redemption in the messy places of your story that you never thought could be redeemed. It is inspiring to me and will be inspiring for you."

Brandon Marshall, NFL Pro Bowl Wide Receiver

"It has been inspiring to watch Jason follow the Lord's call on his life. His family's story of pain, growth, and redemption offer hope to all."

Tony Dungy, Pro Football Hall of Fame Coach and
NBC Sports NFL Analyst

Table of Contents

PART III: TRANSFORMING THE WOUND

PART IV: FORGIVING THE ABUSER

Foreword

by Darryl Strawberry,
Four-time World Series Champion

In May of 2009, I visited ESPN's headquarters in Bristol, Connecticut, to promote my book *Straw: Finding My Way*. There I was introduced to a producer named Jason Romano. He explained that he would be directing me around ESPN throughout the day, guiding me to the different studios for the various television and radio shows on which I would be making appearances for interviews about my book. Jason seemed like a nice guy who I would enjoy being with that day. I soon realized, however, that he would become much more than a guide taking me around to my interviews.

The first thing that Jason and I did was grab breakfast in ESPN's cafeteria. We sat down to eat and began to have a wonderful conversation. He told me about his love for the New York Mets, where I had spent the first seven years of my career, and I was humbled when he shared with me that I was one of his childhood heroes. Before I knew it, we began talking about our spiritual journeys and our shared faith in Jesus Christ. Talking with Jason that morning about our love for the Lord was an encouraging and refreshing way to start the day. God's mercies are new every morning, and on that morning, I knew that my time with Jason was a reflection of God's mercy.

But then the conversation ventured deeper.

We began to talk about pain and addiction.

Addiction is something that I unfortunately know too well. Addictions to cocaine, amphetamines, alcohol, womanizing, and wealth frequently derailed my life and arguably ruined my baseball career. The truth is that the reckless, drug-ridden life I lived should have killed me. But for some reason, God extended grace to me, saved my life, and turned me into an instrument of healing in this world. I guess it was fitting for Jason and me to talk about faith and addiction that morning—on a day that had been arranged for me to share my own broken story in talking about my book at ESPN.

Because of my own struggles, I think that Jason felt comfortable opening up to me about his relationship with his alcoholic father. I could sense that Jason was broken, hurt, and angry. He was desperate for hope and really wanted a solution—some sort of formula that would heal his father. He talked about how much he loved his dad but hated his behavior. What I saw in Jason was a broken son who wanted nothing more than for his dad to get better; yet he was lost and hopeless after decades of unanswered prayers.

Though I did not have a formula to fix Jason's problems or heal his father's alcoholism, I wanted to bring Jason hope and let him know that he was not alone. I understood the depths of his pain. I, too, had hurt my loved ones—my family, friends, and fans—with my horrible decisions and addictions. I understood the complexities of addiction. And I began to realize that my day at ESPN would be about a lot more than talking about my new book. It would be about encouraging Jason.

Throughout the day, Jason and I continued our conversation about addiction in between my interviews. Jason's story resonated with me.

Jason's desire for peace, his hunger to forgive, and his relentless love for his father were all things that deeply touched me. And over the years, when his story would resurface in my mind, I would often text him a simple four-word question: "How is your dad?" I wanted him to know that there was someone who understood addiction who was thinking about his situation and praying for healing.

Now, seven and a half years after meeting Jason Romano on a day when I was sharing my own broken story through the release of my book, it is an honor to write the foreword for Jason's book, as he shares his own broken story about his struggle with forgiveness and his father's struggle with alcoholism.

This book is a must-read for anyone who is struggling to forgive someone or anyone who is trapped in the grip of bitterness. I wish I could have given this book to my own family and friends when I was fighting my own demons.

Jason, I know that it can be scary to share the dark parts of our stories, but know that there is no light without darkness. Through this book, you continue to shine your light—even in something as dark as your father's addiction. Because of this book, the Lord will open many conversations for you to have with others—just like the one you and I had nearly eight years ago.

I have seen God turn my mess into a message that brings hope to others—and he will continue to do the same with you.

Keep shining in the dark.

A Note to the Reader

by Jason Romano

It took a while for me to find the courage to open up about my struggle with forgiving my alcoholic father, and it took me even longer to see that there was true healing—for myself and for others—in sharing my story.

Throughout much of my life, a tension was building—not only between me and my father, but also *within* me. It was a tension—a complexity—that I didn't understand. I often tried to suppress the shame or ignore it, but as emotional as I am, I always seemed to, like a volcano, eventually erupt. What I began to realize, however, was that this fragile area of my life—this deep pain that I tried to hide—was not so much something to be ashamed of but rather was a gateway for healing.

For myself.

For others.

And this book is a culmination of that journey.

What I have attempted to do in this book is reflect upon my own journey toward forgiving my father. In these pages, I have tried to examine what did and didn't work for me. The mistakes I made. The resolve I found. The angst I experienced. The peace that found me.

"The goal of this book is to help you fully feel your emotions and objectively evaluate your pain so that you can truly transform your wound and enter into the peace and freedom of forgiveness."

At times, my story might be difficult to digest because of the apparent horror and intensity in my relationship with my father. I have allowed some of my raw emotion and darkness to exist for the sake of transparency and to perhaps relate more to you, reader, who may be in an unexplainable life situation of your own.

The reality is that most of us have been deeply hurt by someone. In a sense, we will *always* be forgiving that person because of the ever-existing pain. Long-lasting peace sometimes feels so difficult to attain. I learned that my struggle to forgive breached deeper than I could have ever imagined—deep into my emotions, feedback cycles, psyche, thinking patterns, worldview, theology, and spirituality.

Forgiveness is so complex and varied that it is impossible to provide a step-by-step formula for forgiving someone. All I have is my story. And hopefully you can learn a few things about forgiveness from my own journey.

Live to Forgive unfolds in four main sections:

- *Feeling the Pain*—which focuses on embarking on an emotional journey;

- *Evaluating the Trauma*—which explores our ability to analyze our wounds when we've been hurt or betrayed;

- *Transforming the Wound*—which dives into turning our deepest pains into healing for ourselves and for others; and

- *Forgiving the Abuser*—which examines how we can finally let go of bitterness and shame and forgive the debt that is owed to us.

Feeling, evaluating, transforming, and forgiving can be a fluid and complicated process—sometimes happening on multiple levels at the same time. For me, it's a process that continues to this day.

As you read, you'll also notice that the book has several different components:

- *A topical narrative:* The book unfolds chronologically at times but mostly hops around according to the theme of each section. The purpose of this is to drive home the points of feeling, evaluating, transforming, and forgiving.

- *Application sections:* At the end of each chapter are application sections—beginning with a bold, italicized phrase—where I expound the narrative and extract some lessons that can be applied to our journeys of forgiveness.

- *Spiritual chapters:* The final chapter in each of the four parts is meant to venture deeper into the spiritual applications of the section's theme—whether it be feeling, evaluating, transforming, or forgiving. I am writing from a Christian perspective. My faith in Jesus Christ is the most important thing about me. But no matter who is reading, hopefully the spiritual chapters at the end of each section will be meaningful and inspirational.

The goal of this book is to help you fully feel your emotions and objectively evaluate your pain so that you can truly transform your wound and enter into the peace and freedom of forgiveness.

I have titled this book *Live to Forgive* because forgiveness was where I found life in its fullness. As Jesus says in John 10:10, "'The thief comes only to steal and kill and destroy; I have come that they may have life, and have it to the full.'" Bitterness tried to kill my joy and destroy my hope, but in letting go—in forgiveness—I found peace.

I hope this book will encourage you to find that same freedom.

You are not alone.

PART I
FEELING THE PAIN

"When we deny our pain, losses, and feelings year after year, we become less and less human. We transform slowly into empty shells with smiley faces painted on them....But when I began to allow myself to feel a wider range of emotions, including sadness, depression, fear, and anger, a revolution in my spirituality was unleashed."

Peter Scazzero, *Emotionally Healthy Spirituality*

1
Finding Your Father's Secret

The Importance of Feeling

It was the summer of 1984.

I was eleven. My brother Chris was nine. And our little brother Damian was seven.

One Saturday in July, my father said to us, "Get in the car, we are going to the mall."

Upon arriving, my father guided us toward a booth in the mall that had the word "Ticketmaster" plastered in purple italic lettering above the walk-up window.

Dad walked up to the window and, much to our surprise, purchased tickets for all of us to attend a New York Giants versus Philadelphia Eagles game at Veteran's Stadium in the fall.

We were *ecstatic*. It's a moment I'll always remember: The excitement I felt holding that green and black Eagles ticket. The anticipation I had for the game. The pride I had for my father—that he would do this for us, for *me*.

I began counting down the days...

The summer unfolded with lots of backyard football and neighborhood adventures, and before we knew it, it was time for the day we had all been waiting for: the Giants versus the Eagles at the Vet.

It was a chilly, October day in 1984 when we made the four-hour drive from our home in Ravena, New York, to Philadelphia—my dad in the driver's seat, my stepmom, Patty, in the passenger's seat, and my brothers and me in the backseat. I remember pulling into the gigantic parking lot at the Vet, seeing the stadium in the distance, and being mesmerized by the atmosphere—the sea of green and blue in the parking lot as fans from both sides tailgated and prepared to watch their teams battle it out on the gridiron.

Dad parked the car, popped the trunk, and removed his cooler. He reached in, pulled out a Budweiser, cracked it open—*pssssst*—and began to drink.

A couple of hours later, it was time to go into the stadium.

The entire day is still extremely vivid to me. The sights. The smells. The sounds. I remember handing my ticket to the burly man at the entrance and making our way up the circle of ramps toward the infamous "700 Level," a section that is notorious for its hostile, mean-spirited Eagles fans. I remember emerging from the tunnel into the openness and looking down at the splendor of the field—wide-eyed and in awe and feeling as if I was looking behind a curtain, like I was gazing into an entirely new world. I remember taking a seat and flipping through the game program, which had Eagles head coach Dick Vermeil on the cover, and reading each page with childlike wonder.

But unfortunately, I also remember the confusion of that day—the conflicting emotions of happiness and sadness, the excitement and the angst. That's because, by the time we sat down in our seats, my father, Joe Romano, was drunk.

When some people drink, they become goofy or joyfully outgoing. My dad became the opposite. He would go from quiet and reserved to hostile and antagonistic, from kind and jovial to irate and tormenting, from selfless to selfish, and from loving to downright mean. And that day at the game, my dad, a diehard Giants fan, kept getting into verbal fights and spats with the Eagles fans sitting around us—yelling, cursing, antagonizing, and treating total strangers horribly. I remember thinking to myself, *So this is what it's like to go to a game, huh?*

I had never been to a game before, but something deep within me told me that something wasn't right.

As the game unfolded, his anger only got worse. Not only did the matchup feature a big divisional rivalry, but the game was also extremely close—for three quarters, at least. The teams were tied 10-10 entering the final quarter, but Eagles quarterback Ron Jaworski threw two touchdown passes in the fourth to lead Philadelphia to a 24-10 victory.

My dad's anger was on full display. His lack of control made the entire experience terribly confusing.

That particular day epitomized the paradox that is my father—a man who loved his family and wanted to give his sons a special experience, yet a man who interrupted those memories with his alcohol abuse. The day should have brought us all closer together, but instead, it helped create instability and insecurity in my and my brothers' psyches. The day was a representation of both the loving side and the dark side of my dad—a chaos that became our reality.

Unfortunately, things got even worse that day.

After the game, Dad insisted that he was sober enough to drive us home. And all I remember from the next four hours on the road is lots of uncontrolled swerving and unreserved screaming.

"Joe, what're you doing?!" my stepmom kept yelling from the passenger seat.

"Stop it, Dad! Stop it!" my brothers and I kept screaming from the back.

That was the first time in my youth that I felt legitimately frightened and upset under the care of my dad—someone who was supposed to help us to feel safe and secure and loved.

∞

The very thing that should have brought us together is what tore my dad and me apart: *sports*. Much like during the Giants-Eagles game in my youth where I saw my dad's alcoholism on full display in a traumatic way, throughout my life, sports continued to be a place in which my underlying shame and pain rose to the top. Sports became a battleground where my dad's shame, stemming from his addiction, was revealed, and my deepest pains, stemming from his abuse, were also revealed. Like when my Dallas Cowboys played against his New York Giants. Or my New York Mets faced his St. Louis Cardinals.

These matchups oftentimes became outlets for us to project our unprocessed hurts onto one another. Why? Because the truth is that I was failing to deal with my pain in a healthy way, and it had to come out somehow.

As I got older, I sometimes rooted against my father's teams because I wanted him to suffer, and I knew how much a Giants or Cardinals loss would crush him. Looking back, I can see that doing this was an attempt of mine to deal with the pain—all the emotions swarming around within me, stemming from all the hurt my dad caused when he was drunk, which I will dive into later.

I guess it's fitting that sports became such a battleground for my father and me. Not only was sports a door into the complicated realm where I caught a glimpse of the dark world of my dad's alcoholism—where I was confronted with an aching feeling within me that there was something deeply wrong with him—but it was also through sports that Dad began his forty-plus year drinking problem.

My dad liked going to bars, being around people at the bars, and watching sports at the bars. The bar was his safe place, I think—because at twenty-eight years old, he was already divorced with three kids (a split-up that partially had to do with his festering addiction). The divorce happened when I was five years old, and I unfortunately have no memory of my parents being together. I'm no therapist, but as I evaluate all of this, I get the feeling that my dad was already beginning to feel like a failure at that point. At the bar, however, he didn't feel judged for his drinking because everyone else was drinking.

The alcohol helped my dad numb his pain. Sports also helped him escape and distract himself from who he was becoming.

But like most alcoholics, my dad's drinking didn't stay at the bar. And most of my childhood memories of Dad's drunken stupors were connected to sports in some way.

There were the Saturdays during the spring and summer that were filled with Little League baseball. I can still remember the exciting feeling of slipping on that Little League uniform as a nine-year-old boy and taking the mound as a pitcher. And though baseball was my favorite sport to play, there was often an intruder at my games: my drunken father. My dad was very vocal when he drank—not only toward me but also toward the umpires. I cringed on the mound whenever I heard my dad's voice.

Then there were the Sundays during the fall and winter—a time to watch football but also a time for my dad to feed his addiction. One time, I remember the Giants losing on a last-second touchdown, and my dad was so angry in his drunkenness that he picked up a pot in the house and fired it at the television. The pot broke. Dirt went everywhere. He didn't care. He was violent. It was scary.

My father and I did have one team in common: the Boston Celtics. We *loved* Larry Bird, and some of my fondest memories with my dad in my youth involved watching the Celtics with him on the Sunday CBS "Game of the Week." Throughout my life, watching the Celtics was an opportunity for us to relate to one another and connect, despite the existing tension in our relationship. Although sports became a battle-ground for us, the Celtics were always a safe place.

The truth is that my brothers and I have always loved our father. And we could tell that he loved us—when he was sober, at least. We naturally gravitated toward him, like any son would with his dad. I think the fact that my brothers and I all love sports might be a reflection of our deep craving for connection and intimacy with our father. The fact that we all chose different teams to root for might be a reflection of the tension that was always there. The fact that I inherited my dad's love for the Celtics—that we always had this connection no matter how complicated things became—might be a reflection of how I never gave up on him.

Overall, sports was arguably what Dad cared about most in his life, so maybe the underlying feeling in all of us was that if we could meet him on that level, then perhaps we could gain his affection.

∽

Needless to say, my father's Jekyll-and-Hyde existence made our childhood extremely unstable. There was always a longing for a father who acted like a father should. A deep unsettledness that something wasn't right.

Adding to the instability was the fact that both Mom and Dad re-married different people in 1985, when I was eleven years old. I don't remember much about Mom's wedding. What I remember about Dad's is that he had me stand up as his best man. This is a vivid picture, I think, of how his alcoholism was pushing away his friends and family and preventing relational intimacy.

Both my parents' second marriages also ended in divorce—Mom's marriage ended because the man she married was physically abusive, and Dad's marriage ended because of his alcoholism. Our tumultuous childhoods were replete with marriages ending and relationships falling apart—and through it all was our dad, a man who we loved and looked up to and whose love toward us was always a roller-coaster ride. It's crazy to think that having a loving father hinged on whether or not he was drinking that day.

Luckily there was at least *some* stability—a form of consistency—in our childhoods.

And that is mostly because of my mom, Linda. In our formative years of middle school and high school, Mom sacrificed everything for her boys. She worked multiple jobs. She paid the bills. Took us where we needed to go. Supported us. We received what every child deserves from a mother.

That feeling of safety and stability was also in our relationship with our grandparents (my father's parents), who we called Nana and Pa. If it weren't for them, I know that Chris, Damian, and I wouldn't be who we are today. In many ways, they were our second set of parents. Though my dad was the metaphorical starting quarterback, he was always inactive because of his alcoholism; Pa, however, came in as the backup quarterback and filled in for my father perfectly. He became the father I never had.

Living only a couple of blocks away from my mom, Nana and Pa provided the assistance their daughter-in-law needed as a single mother. Though Mom had full custody, we spent a lot of time at Nana and Pa's house, especially on the weekends. They took us to every single game and practice we needed to go to. And not only did they love us unconditionally in my father's stead; they also spoiled us! They bought us nice clothes and sneakers and any toy we ever wanted. Most importantly, just like my mother, they showed us that safety and love existed.

What's interesting about my grandparents' relationship with my father, their only child, is that they let him live in their house after the divorce. My dad took full advantage of this, and my grandparents never had the guts to kick him out—even years later when he was *still* living with them. I think my dad's alcoholism prevented him from ever really "growing up." Though my grandparents' presence during our childhood ultimately helped to stabilize us and position us for success, they enabled my dad's bad behaviors because of their inability to create boundaries with their son. My dad always had a place to live and never really hit rock bottom.

I can only imagine how difficult and confusing it had to have been for Nana and Pa to see their son waste his life. After all, Dad had been an exemplary son throughout his childhood, high school, and college years. He was responsible and driven. He was smart, too—and he would be the first to tell you. He made good grades in school, making honors in both high school and college. To this day, he is one of the smartest men I know. Dad can recall exact dates, statistics, and specifics in his memories—especially when it comes to sports. I will often talk to him as if I am consulting a historian and ask him all kinds of sports questions about specific players, seasons, and stats. I get my photographic memory from him—there is no doubt about that. But it's always been baffling to me that my father could be so intelligent and yet so dumb and reckless at the same time.

∞

Amidst all this turmoil in my youth, what I witnessed growing up was an unemotional family, except when my dad would drink. My grandparents, as kind and loving as they were, harbored a great deal of anger and sadness—but they never expressed it. They kept their emotions buried deep down inside. These emotional tendencies of my father and my grandparents were handed down to my brothers and me. We were either very reactionary, like my father, expressing ourselves through anger and rage; or we were very passive, like my grandparents, suppressing the pain that we did not want to confront.

My mother was the only one who presented us with any kind of emotional awareness or agility. When my brothers and I were in grade school and middle school, Mom decided to take us to counseling. Mom had gone to therapy herself because of the scars my dad and her second husband had caused, and she had a general understanding of some of the long-term psychological effects that my dad's alcoholism could have on his children.

We reluctantly went with Mom to the counselor on Wednesday nights. Memories from those counseling sessions are vivid to me. The offices were on the top floor of a thirty-story building in Albany. Though I didn't realize it at the time, now that lengthy elevator ride feels symbolic of the long emotional journeys we were embarking on in our lives—the long, hard work that it would take to transcend the hurt.

In the waiting room, gentle jazz and piano played through the speakers, but my brothers and I were always loud and obnoxious. Mom would hush us, over and over, and eventually the therapist, an Italian man named Tony, would emerge from a back room. There was always an awkward exchange between us and the family who was leaving Tony's office. I remember always thinking, "I wonder what's wrong with them."

Tony's office had a big couch with two chairs on each side. He would sit in front of us, as if it were an American Idol audition. Mom always cried during the sessions. I'm not sure if we were able to get in touch with our feelings then, but Mom showed us that it was okay to reveal them in such a setting. We didn't know it at the time, but seeds were planted then that later helped us deal with our emotions

∞

Much of my childhood and adolescent years, however, were reflective of that terrifying car ride on the way back to Ravena after the Giants-Eagles game. Chaotic. Confusing. Complicated. In the car, but not in control of its direction. With your family, but knowing deep within you that something wasn't right. Feeling so much confusion and anxiety, but not knowing how to express it. Trapped in some sort of purgatory, with no idea how to find heaven, health, and happiness.

Now I can see that the fear and angst I experienced that day as a child were emotions that served as gateways for deeper insights into reality. My emotions were internal sirens letting me know that something in my life was horribly wrong. They were road signs pointing me toward a greater awareness of what was unfolding in my life and within my soul.

∞

Your emotions can be insights into reality.

In their book *The Cry of the Soul*, authors Dan Allender and Tremper Longman explain the importance of our emotions: "Ignoring our emotions is turning our back on reality. Listening to our emotions ushers us into reality. And reality is where we meet God....Emotions are the language of the soul. They are the cry that gives the heart a voice."

Though I had little idea what all of this meant, say, when I was a terrified child watching Dad swerve all over the road because he was drunk, this "emotional awareness" became one of the most important journeys in my life. The emotions that always welled up within me, as they related to the abuse stemming from Dad's alcoholism, pulled me deeper into two realities:

- *An external reality*—the unresolved issues in my dad's life and the problems they caused for those he loved, which I *couldn't* control; and

- *An internal reality*—the unresolved issues in my own life and the problems they were causing for me, which I *could* begin to acknowledge and work through.

The challenge is that emotions are typically downplayed as misleading and unimportant in our culture. In our society, men and women are both told—directly or subliminally—to hide their emotions. Expressing sadness is often viewed as a weakness. And so we naturally create facades to hide what we do not want others to see.

Even when I became a Christian in the early 2000s, internal troubles like depression, sadness, or anxiety were sometimes viewed as things that stemmed from a problem with a person's relationship with God. As a result, many people downplayed what they felt. This led to avoidance, detachment, and suppression. However, in moving toward forgiveness, it's vital to allow ourselves to feel our emotions.

"Though my emotions are not always reality, I have learned that my emotions can point me toward reality. Especially reoccurring emotions. Our emotions can be an enter sign for the internal work that we have to do or an exit sign for a situation that we need to get out of."

Though my emotions are not always reality, I have learned that my emotions can point me *toward* reality. Especially reoccurring emotions. Our emotions can be an enter sign for the internal work that we have to do or an exit sign for a situation that we need to get out of. I believe that mending a broken relationship can only occur with an awareness and acknowledgment of the internal chaos and havoc—our emotions.

If we bury our emotions, it's easier to live in an unnatural reality. And for a long time, this is what I did. Learning how to listen to my emotions was a struggle for me.

2

Huddled on the Bathroom Floor

Allowing Yourself to Feel

As I ventured through my childhood, the emotions that I felt eventually reached their boiling point.

A few years after the Giants-Eagles game, my dad planned a trip for us to attend a New York Mets-St. Louis Cardinals game at Shea Stadium in Queens, New York City. Once more, my feelings leading up to the game were of pure joy and excitement. The Cardinals were his favorite team. The Mets were mine. And this was during the Mets' prime when they had two of my baseball heroes, Darryl Strawberry and Dwight Gooden. And most importantly, it was the first time that I as a teenager had planned to go to a game with just my dad. No one else. Just the two of us, traveling to the city to watch our favorite teams together in person.

The night before the game, I was at my grandparents' house watching baseball on their television when Dad came home. I could tell that something was vastly different about him. He was combative, vocal, and loud. I could smell the alcohol.

He was *wasted.*

My heart sunk, and my mind went to a dark, sad place.

The best word I can think of to describe my feelings is betrayal.

We were on the eve of a day that I had been excited for, and my dad couldn't even hold it together for one night. And believe me, I knew by then how everything would go. Once my dad started drinking, it often took him days to stop. I knew he would continue drinking on the bus…and at the ballpark…and on the way home. I quickly realized I no longer wanted to go to the game.

I found myself asking my dad, "Why are you doing this? Why is this happening?"

He assured me that we could still go to the game, but I no longer wanted to. If alcohol was going to be in the picture, I wanted no part of being around my dad. The fact that he was hammered the night before we were supposed to leave, in my mind, was his way of showing me that he did not love me or care about me.

I hated it when he was drunk. And he knew I hated it.

I could feel something boiling up within me.

Something within me burst, and I began to yell and scream uncontrollably at my dad.

"How could you do this to me the night before? You need help! You're crazy!"

To try and escape, I fled to a bathroom. I sat down on the toilet, and I kept crying, shaking my head, and saying, "I can't believe it, I can't believe it."

I was surprised by the sudden, reactive emotional state that had taken control of my entire being. By retreating to a different room, I felt like I'd put a boundary up between me and my dad—this person I loved who kept hurting me so deeply.

Dad followed me, and our screaming match continued—this time separated by the bathroom door.

For perhaps the first time, my anger toward him was unreserved. At other times, his alcohol abuse had confused me (like in Philadelphia), but this time my emotion was easy to pinpoint: *I was angry.*

Rage washed over me like a flood. I eventually moved from the toilet seat to the floor: a reflection, perhaps, of the hopelessness that I felt. It was a long way from the floor of that bathroom to the counseling offices on the thirtieth story: a symbol, perhaps, of the emotional journey that lay ahead of me.

Years before, I might not have known what was right or wrong, but at that time, I knew something was wrong and unjust about his conduct.

"C'mon, Jay, come on out," my dad begged.

"I'm not coming out!" I screamed. "I'm staying in here! I need you to get away from me!"

It was so chaotic that Nana and Pa also got involved and began pleading with me to come out of the bathroom, hoping to downplay everything.

"Jay, you gotta come out," I remember Pa saying to me through the bathroom door.

"Pa, I can't deal with Dad," I said. "I wanted to go to a baseball game, and he can't even stay sober for me."

I guess you could say that was the root of it.

What was I worth if my father chose alcohol over me, time after time?

When people used to ask why I didn't drink, I would always say, "Because my dad chose the bottle over his sons."

∞

Allow yourself to feel whatever confusing thing is disrupting you.

Aren't we all just frightened children, screaming and crying on the floor in a lonely bathroom?

Most of us have had someone in our lives who was supposed to make us feel safe and secure but instead made us feel the exact opposite—a family member, a teacher, a coach, a spiritual director, a significant other, a spouse, or a friend. I'm sure there have also unfortunately been times when we have made others feel unsafe or insecure.

Whatever the case, the picture of a cowering child, screaming and crying in the confines of a bathroom, is an emotional state that I've returned to time and time again throughout my life.

The flood of confusing emotions: Panic. Fear. Hatred. Betrayal.

At the time, it was an array of things I had never felt before.

So what should you do if you feel hurt or wounded and experience deeply confusing emotions? I believe that you should allow yourself to do exactly what a lot of children naturally do when they are confronted with something that disrupts their sense of stability: find a safe, healthy place, or someone who you feel safe around, and then allow yourself to feel it. *All of it.*

Cry. Scream. Shout.

Let it out. It's all part of the process.

You are not weak for feeling. Your ability to be in touch with your emotions is actually what makes you strong. It is a daring, courageous thing to allow yourself to feel exactly what you are feeling.

Yes, it can be uncomfortable to allow yourself to feel. But you often must first move *through* the pain before you find joy at the bottom. You must first move *through* the grief before you find hope at the bottom.

Moving toward forgiveness does not mean suppressing your emotions. Many will flippantly say that they forgive someone, but their "forgiveness" is actually a way of detaching themselves from what they feel. I did this for many years. To fully forgive, we first must delve into the pain that the abuser or perpetrator caused.

"To act like nothing is wrong might seem less disruptive, but it actually does the opposite of what you think it does; it sets you up for an eruption down the road. It's not okay to pretend that nothing is wrong."

It is okay to be confused, especially when you first become aware of the abuse, wrongdoing, or pain that was inflicted upon you. It is okay to not know what to do with your emotions. It is okay to lock yourself in a bathroom, drop to the floor, and scream. Though you might feel as if you are out of control, it is actually normal. Your confusion proves that you are human, that you have a big heart, and that you care about the person who is hurting you. To act like nothing is wrong might seem less disruptive, but it actually does the opposite of what you think it does; it sets you up for an eruption down the road. It's not okay to pretend that nothing is wrong.

And most importantly, your inner restlessness and discontentment with a situation can show that you care about yourself. And that's a good thing.

3

When My Brothers Wanted to Kill My Dad

The Validity of Anger

One of the main characters in the 1986 film *Hoosiers*—which tells the story of a small-town Indiana high school basketball team that won a state championship—is an alcoholic named Shooter (played by Dennis Hopper). The head coach of the basketball team is a man with a checkered coaching past named Norman Dale (played by Gene Hackman), and he offers Shooter a spot on the bench as an assistant coach under one caveat: that he sobers up.

Not only would it be inappropriate for Shooter to be intoxicated around impressionable high schoolers, but Shooter's son, Everett, also plays on the team; Coach Dale tells Shooter that his drunken actions are embarrassing his son.

Shooter sobers up for much of the season, but he caves to the bottle's temptation the day of the sectional final and stumbles onto the court in the middle of the game, yelling at an official and waving his arms around like a maniac. Shooter, who is nearly falling over, has to be escorted out of the gymnasium. (That scene has always struck a chord because it reminds me of my dad at our sporting events.) Everett is obviously humiliated by his father's display and fumes with anger. Coach Dale puts his arm around Everett and says, "You keep your head in the game."

But throughout the course of the game, as the reality of what happened sets in, Everett becomes more and more upset. Eventually he explodes and punches a player on the opposing team, causing a fight that eventually leads to Everett being thrown into a trophy case, bloodying up his shoulder.

Like Everett, my brothers and I were always on the verge of exploding. There was always that voice in my head saying, "Keep your head in the game," but sometimes, like an internal volcano, my emotions boiled over and affected my actions.

I share these stories of anger in this chapter not because my brothers and I always handled our anger well but to show that our anger was always there.

When something like abuse or addiction is at play, strong emotions—emotions that need to be experienced, acknowledged, and evaluated—always seem to be beneath the surface.

For my brothers and I, the internal volcano in each of us was always boiling, and we were often only one scenario away from erupting.

When we were pushed too far, destruction occurred.

∞

Damian once shared a story with me about when he and Chris were living at Nana's and Pa's in their upstairs apartment in the late 1990s. (At the time, I was living in Guilderland, New York, a town right outside of Albany.)

Late one evening, Dad stumbled into Nana's and Pa's house while Chris and Damian were watching *Austin Powers: The Spy Who Shagged Me*. As my brothers recall it, Damian was pretty high and was having an interesting evening.

Anyway, by this point, Dad's drinking had festered into a twenty-year cycle of alcoholism—and it caused him to frequently verbally abuse the people he loved, like his sons. He never physically abused us, but we were often victims of his verbal abuse. And whenever we fired words back at him, it only fueled his response—riddled with expletives, name-calling, and downright mean attacks.

And so on that evening with Chris and Damian, Dad started doing what he usually did: provoking them and cursing them out. Chris eventually snapped, and Damian had to physically hold him back. This is still baffling to me, as Chris is one of the most levelheaded men you could ever meet.

Tempers flared.

The tension rose.

Nana and Pa heard the commotion and came out to see what was happening.

Dad continued to antagonize his sons—calling them names and

making personal jabs at them. Damian then lost control, charging at Dad and shoving him to the floor. Damian says that this was the first time he had ever laid a finger on Dad in a violent way. Dad looked up at him with a terrified look in his eye—in disbelief of what his own son had done.

Damian says that something within him had flared up and that he'd truly felt like killing Dad. The volcano had burst within him. And it wasn't just an emotional reaction or one that was connected to his marijuana usage. Damian says there was logic behind it. He wanted to free us all from the misery Dad was causing in our lives. Damian looked at Nana and Pa and said, "If you don't call the cops, I'm going to kill your son."

A cop eventually arrived at the house and the policeman explained, "I really can't take your father away. Getting drunk isn't illegal."

Chris bluntly said, "I'm going to tell you this right now: if you don't take him away, my brother and I are probably going to beat him to death. Put him in a cell for a night. Please. Anything."

The cop paused and then said, "Did he hit you?"—which was basically his way of telling Chris and Damian that if they said "yes," then he could take Dad away.

"Yep, he hit us," Chris said affirmatively.

And the cop took Dad away, forcing him to spend the night in the county jail.

∞

Though I never physically laid a hand on Dad, my anger with him was often bursting at the seams.

This anger was usually triggered by one of his phone calls—which he started routinely making to me, Chris, and Damian as his alcoholism worsened throughout my twenties. Sometimes he called us when he was sober (and those were good, healthy conversations), but mostly he called us when he was drunk. I have no idea why he did this, because it only had a negative effect on our relationship with him. Had he managed his alcoholism—keeping his drunkenness to himself and staying sober when he was with us—our relationship with him would've been a lot healthier and easier. The less we knew, the better. The unfortunate thing is that we always knew way more than we needed to know.

I'm theorizing here, but I think Dad had a deep insecurity about feeling unwanted and unloved, so maybe calling us while he was drunk was subconsciously a desperate cry for attention—a plea for us to love him and accept him in his most vulnerable state as he wrestled with the defining struggle of his life: alcohol.

Most of the time, however, those calls only upset us. We would get angry at him, and then he would snap back at us. And when we ignored him, his temper reached new heights. Many times he'd call us the next day to apologize because he'd know that he'd said some bad things.

The calls seemed to increase whenever I was out of Dad's reach—like when I went to college three hours away or when I moved to Connecticut for my job. Sometimes the only way for my dad to stay in touch was through a phone call—especially when he got his license suspended or revoked due to his multiple DWIs.

Sadly, calls from Dad continued into my late thirties when I had a family of my own. Sometimes it felt like Dad was playing a cruel game with me—trying to pin me in a corner with a phone call so that he could hurt me on the other line. There was always a sinking feeling in my chest when I heard his slurred voiced on the other line. Though I had grown accustomed to his alcoholism by adulthood, the void he caused, the wound he left, and the hope I had for change were always there. That hope, however, was hard to hold onto. And those calls were reminders of the perpetual problems that existed in our family.

During adulthood, I usually remained somewhat composed when Dad called me. I was in control of the relationship by that point. Sometimes I would hang up on him. Sometimes I'd ask him not to call me until he was sober. I knew what I could and couldn't handle. But one day, like the story Damian and Chris shared with me about when they wanted to physically beat him to death, I lost my cool.

I had stopped picking up the phone one day because Dad had gotten drunk and kept calling me. And that's when he left his standard voice message that went something along the lines of, "You're not gonna pick up the phone? You know who you are? You're a coward. You're a son of a b**** and an a**hole and a mother-f***er…And the Cowboys are a piece of s***."

But then the voicemail got worse. He brought my family into it, also attaching their names to a sting of expletives.

And at that moment, I went into all-out attack mode. Throughout the course of my life, it wasn't uncommon for him to sometimes say, "F*** you, Jason," in his drunken states. Though no son should have to hear that, I could take it. But talking like that about my family was a different story. It sent me over the edge. That's when he crossed the line, and I felt like I could never forgive him for it.

The next time he called, I picked up the phone and laid into him. For at least ten minutes straight, I yelled and screamed. Though this time I had more control, it was as if I was once again on the bathroom floor, overcome by anger. Dad was silent on the other end as I berated him. He was probably shocked—like when Damian pushed him down. I'd never lashed out at him like that before.

"Are you done?" he eventually asked, quietly.

I thought about it, then said, "No, I'm not done yet," and continued to scold him for several more minutes.

$$\infty$$

Anger and hatred are okay—but they must be moved through.

My brothers and I are not proud of how we sometimes responded to Dad in his drunken states, but our festering anger was the emotional norm for us. What strikes me most about the movie *Hoosiers* that I referenced earlier, is that Coach Norman Dale's belief in Shooter—and the opportunity he gave him to be an assistant coach—was a boost of confidence that eventually helped Shooter move toward sobriety. Coach Dale's belief in Shooter ultimately helped Shooter also believe in himself; Couch Dale's hope in Shooter was the initial wind in his sails that helped him to leave the dock of his alcoholism.

In many senses, I think that Coach Dale saw himself in Shooter because he too had a broken past. While coaching college basketball, Coach Dale had lost his temper and hit one of his players, something that resulted in him losing his job and disqualifying him from ever coaching at that level again. That's how he found himself at little Hickory High School—the only place he could get a coaching job.

Coach Dale believed that Shooter deserved a second chance because he himself had received a second chance; he believed that Shooter could change because his athletic director had believed that he'd changed.

Often it takes an awareness of the brokenness in ourselves to see the brokenness in others—and to meet them in their struggles.

My dad's alcoholism, however, was very difficult for me and my brothers to understand. Coach Dale could give Shooter a second chance because he had, in a sense, walked in his shoes as he had wrestled with his own past. But we had never walked in my dad's shoes.

> "Sometimes it takes a heightened emotion like anger to finally realize that boundaries are needed. Those who don't get angry over the harm that has been done to them or who aren't willing to create boundaries might not have a good understanding of their self-worth, their wholeness as a child of God."

We were too close to the situation and too wounded by it. Our perspective aligned with Everett's in *Hoosiers*—we were embarrassed, humiliated, and angry; we believed our dad to be a loser and a drunk. We hoped he would change, but by the time we got to adulthood, we were very calloused and used to being let down.

The interesting thing about anger is that it usually rises out of something deeper. It usually masks something else—usually a deeper emotion like sadness or shame. I'm not sure if my anger masked anything, but I know that my anger rose from something deeper.

I lashed out at Dad on the phone because of my inner feelings of disappointment. He was repuncturing old wounds by allowing his alcoholism to intrude upon the deepest and most important parts of my life: my family.

Though I think it's important to be aware of what anger might be masking and of what anger is rising out of from deep within, I also think there can be some value in anger. It can reveal things inside of us that we have yet to deal with. It can make a statement to the abuser and reinforce boundaries that have been breached. Our anger should be carefully managed, but it shouldn't be suppressed.

Sometimes it takes a heightened emotion like anger to finally realize that boundaries are needed. Those who don't get angry over the harm that has been done to them or who aren't willing to create boundaries might not have a good understanding of their self-worth, their wholeness as a child of God.

Psychologist Leon Seltzer echoes these sentiments in an article titled "The Rarely Recognized Upside of Anger" in *Psychology Today*: "So what's so positive about your annoyance or umbrage? Simply that in various circumstances when you're not getting what you want—and think you *deserve* (or the exact opposite)—your angry reaction represents a vital affirmation of self-worth."

The most difficult challenge in managing anger is to not dehumanize the person who has angered us—something that I often failed to do when it came to my dad. He was wrestling with enough of his own self-worth issues; he didn't need me to yell at him the way I did. But maybe he *did* need to see a glimpse of my anger so that he wouldn't continue to leave insulting voicemails.

Anger is a tricky thing, and the way it should be expressed depends on the situation. It's interesting to me as a Christian that Jesus seems to show his anger a number of times in the Bible. This most notably occurs when Jesus turns over the tables of the money-changers in the temple (Matthew 21)—angry that what was meant to be a "house of prayer" had been turned into a "den of robbers." Jesus also shows his anger when confronting the Pharisees on their hypocrisy, as they had turned the beauty of a relationship with God into bounding laws and codes to boost their own egos.

Through Jesus's example, we see that anger is a part of our reality and our inner complexity as humans—and that there are things in this world that we *should* get angry about. Interestingly, one might argue that Jesus's conduct toward the money-changers in the temple and the Pharisees wasn't exactly respectful and might have been somewhat dehumanizing—but I also think that it was *loving*. Jesus cared so much about people's approach to faith that he knew he needed to make a statement in order to move the stubborn-hearted people toward change and a new level of intimacy with God.

Christ's approach and intentions might be a good gauge for how we choose to express our anger, though I also think it's important to remember that he was the Son of God and we are not. He was sinless, and we are not. Is our anger selfish—rooted in vengeance, entitlement, or self-righteousness? Are we responding to a situation in a calculated way or in an out-of-control way? Is there a deeper issue behind our anger?

Those are questions we all need to ponder as we move toward forgiveness, allowing ourselves to feel in the process.

4

The Speech and the Void

Beneath the Anger: Sadness and Grief

The anger I explored in the last chapter was a mechanism that usually masked a deeper emotion: sadness stemming from a void. The lack of having a reliable father created a void within me—a hole that only seemed to get bigger the more complicated our relationship became. As I ventured through my late teens and early twenties, I tried to mature, but I had an ever-expanding void within me. It was painful and confusing.

Reminders of this void often came through tears, the obvious by-product of sadness. What's interesting is that I'm not much of a crier. I'm an emotional person, but I rarely cry. However, as I reflect on the dozen or so times in my life when I *did* cry, almost all of them were related in one way or another to the void Dad left within me. Parental issues run deep, affecting the very core of our beings.

For example, because of Dad's drinking, I sometimes had a hard time navigating the social scene at Cayuga Community College— where I enrolled after high school because they had the best two-year broadcasting program in the state. My good buddy and roommate, Ed, who I've been friends with since I was six years old, used to host parties at our duplex in college. Interestingly, our place was *the* go-to spot for parties on campus. Leave it to me, someone who *never* drank and the son of an alcoholic, to live at the epicenter of college parties at Cayuga. Thankfully, no one at school judged me for not drinking, and they truly seemed to accept me for who I was—without me even having to explain my family background to them. I think our apartment was such a hotspot for hangouts because Ed had learned how to be a hip-hop deejay and really knew how to throw a good party. It seemed like we had people over at our apartment almost every night.

47

At these parties, however, I noticed that I would become very uncomfortable whenever people became severely intoxicated. I was fine being around the drinking, but whenever people lost control, I would feel uneasy and would sometimes shut down or go to my room for the night. Now I can see that this trigger was connected to my childhood.

The worst trigger I experienced at one of these parties was when I had an altercation with an intoxicated guy named Troy, a guy I hardly knew. He was walking up the stairs in our two-story duplex, and I was walking down the stairs and casually said to him, "What's up, man?"

He must have thought I said something else because he angrily replied, "What did you say?"

"Yo, what's up?" I repeated.

"I'll show you what's up," he said, and then he punched me right in the face.

Obviously, I was shocked and stunned. I didn't even have a relationship with this guy. And he was in *my* apartment!

I immediately removed myself from the situation and walked into a room where Ed and some of my good friends were gathered. Ed could tell that something was wrong and immediately asked, "Jay, what's going on?"

"Ed, someone just punched me," I said.

And suddenly, the tears started uncontrollably flowing. I had no idea why I was crying or what was going on because he hadn't even hit me that hard. There I was, a grown man crying at a college party that we were hosting. Needless to say, I didn't feel very "cool" that day. But my friends were great throughout the whole ordeal. They crowded around me and vowed to find Troy and kick him out of the party, which they did.

Little did I know at the time that my tears had to do with much, much more.

A wound that went deeper than I could possibly imagine.

A void that was wider than I could have fathomed.

∞

Getting punched at the party brought back old trauma, as it reminded me of my dad's abuse in my childhood when he would get intoxicated and out-of-control—when incomprehensible situations would suddenly unfold. And a half-decade later, my inner sadness blindsided me in a very unexpected way: at Nana's and Pa's fiftieth wedding anniversary party.

To celebrate their fifty years of marriage, we had rented out a banquet room at a nearby restaurant and had invited about forty people to the party. All of Nana's and Pa's closest friends and family members were there—that is, except for their own son and only child, Joe Romano. Sometimes Dad was hesitant to go to functions like that with family because of the overwhelming sense of shame and failure that seemed to consume him. He often felt like others were judging him, which was probably true. Regardless, my brothers and I felt that his own parents' fiftieth anniversary was something that he should've manned up and been at.

As my brothers and I sat at a table, we felt the void of our father's absence—once again a poignant reminder of the emptiness we had always felt within ourselves. This was also when I had first started to date my future wife, Dawn. We had only been together for a couple months, and though I had told her about my complicated relationship with my father, this was her first personal experience seeing my emotions that stemmed from the void I had always felt.

Being the oldest grandchild, I was asked to stand up and say a couple words about Nana and Pa, the most loving, generous people I have ever known. A couple who opened their home to us in our youth. A couple who gave us safety and stability throughout their son's alcohol abuse. A couple who adapted to the unexpected rise of their son's alcoholism and became parental figures to us. A couple who helped make me and my brothers who we are today.

When I stood up to speak, something strange washed over me. The combination of my overwhelming gratitude for them and the inner sadness I felt over my father not being there that day—a reflection of his constant absence in our lives—paralyzed me. I tried to open my mouth and talk, but I couldn't. I kept choking up. It was the weirdest thing. I had no idea what was happening.

My mother, who understood what was going on, spoke up and tried to defuse the situation with humor. She hated seeing me in such a broken state. I joked with my mom a little bit in front of everyone, which helped to break the ice, and then I transitioned into my speech. Thanks to Mom, I escaped the moment without breaking down in front of all my friends and family and my new girlfriend. But the scene accurately depicted the emotional state that my brothers and I were always in—only one moment away from a breakdown, only one moment away from coming face-to-face with the lifelong void within ourselves.

∽

I mentioned in the first chapter that my mother used to take my brothers and me to a counselor named Tony in our youth. Well, years later, after going through a difficult breakup post-college, before I had met Dawn, some of my strange memories from my childhood with Tony resurfaced. For some reason, I asked my mom if she could reconnect me with him. Though I had little awareness of all the emotions swirling around within me at the time, deep down I think that I knew what I needed to do because of the seed Mom had planted. I was lost, frantic, broken, and looking for answers. I needed a guide to help me sift through all the confusing things within me.

Though my breakup might have prompted me to give Tony a call, what I realized when I met with him was that my confusing emotions went much deeper than my romantic struggles. Honestly, I don't remember much about the actual session, but looking back, I feel that much of my insecurity and instability at that age stemmed from a relational lack. In other words, most of the insecurities I had in my life were related to my dad in some way.

Trauma in our lives amplifies the natural disappointments and rejections we experience. These feelings can be especially confusing if we aren't aware of where the pain is *really* coming from. This went all the way back to middle school and high school.

For example, in middle school, I remember feeling a heightened sense of inadequacy in the classroom. Academics were not my strong suit. Though I made the basketball team in seventh grade, which was a big confidence boost, my mom forced me to quit the team when my report card revealed that I'd scored a fifty-five percent in science and a fifty-eight percent in English. I was humiliated having to tell my coach and my teammates that I could no longer play.

My point, however, is that, although struggling in school might be a fairly normal thing, my deep feeling of inadequacy stemmed from the many times in my childhood where my dad placed alcohol above his family. So my natural feeling of inadequacy in my academic struggles was even more personal, because I grew up always believing I was inadequate because of Dad's decision-making.

In high school, the trend was similar. Though academics continued to be something that I had to pour a lot of my energy into just to get by, a heightened sense of inadequacy stemmed from my relationships. I was a very sensitive kid. I remember being teased when someone found out that I had a notebook of hand-kept stats of my favorite basketball player, Larry Bird, that I would tally during basketball games. I also remember feeling humiliated the night of my junior prom when I put into motion an extravagant plan to ask my date to be my girlfriend— only to be ditched at the dance for another guy. I was so humiliated that I left the dance and just walked home. I guess it was just another example of someone who I cared for abandoning me in an important moment.

Again, these were normal things that a lot of high schoolers go through—a little bit of teasing and a little bit of rejection—but because of my traumatic childhood, I had a desperate desire for acceptance. I'd so rarely felt accepted by Dad. This made these seemingly silly situations all the more complicated.

Our childhoods seem to affect *everything*.

Past trauma always seeps into unexpected places within ourselves and into seemingly unrelated circumstances.

And it was no different when the girl I was dating post-college and I broke up. I was hurt and disappointed. But my longing for affection and acceptance and stability and commitment came from a much deeper place: the father I never had.

After my counseling session with Tony, I returned to my car and felt a sense of relief. It had felt amazing to get out some of the emotions I had been feeling and to have someone sitting across from me who was committed to listening to me. Before putting the keys in the ignition, I found myself uncontrollably starting to bawl. I thought to myself, "What is happening?"

But it felt good.

∞

Sadness and grief are essential in bringing awareness to the depth of the wound.

Psychiatrist and neuroscience expert Daniel Siegel uses the acronym COAL—Curiosity, Openness, Acceptance, and Love—to describe the qualities of mindfulness, which I also think is a posture we should have toward ourselves as we evaluate our emotions and thinking patterns.

With a COAL stance, there is no judgment and no expectation—it is an all-embracing attitude on the journey of introspection. Every emotion serves a purpose. Whenever something inside us wells up and confuses us or disrupts us, it serves as a lens to help us to see reality more clearly.

Anger (or any secondary emotion) can take us deeper into the truth of that reality, and fully processing the nuances of sadness and grief can help us go on our own personal journeys and find acceptance and joy at the bottom of the pain.

It can be scary to allow ourselves to feel. Men often feel societal pressure to be strong and confident and "have it all together"; therefore, we sometimes feel a sense of guilt and shame in allowing ourselves to cry or show any other vulnerability. It's uncomfortable. It's new. Sometimes it feels like there is something wrong with us.

> *"Anger (or any secondary emotion) can take us deeper into the truth of that reality, and fully processing the nuances of sadness and grief can help us go on our own personal journeys and find acceptance and joy at the bottom of the pain."*

When I cried at the college party after getting punched and at my grandparents' fiftieth anniversary while giving a speech and in my car after therapy, I was absolutely terrified. I was not in touch with the extent of my sadness and grief. But I can also say that each time it felt good.

Similarly, in Paul Young's bestselling novel *The Shack*, the God character known as "Papa" says these profound words about grief: "Don't ever discount the wonder of your tears. They can be healing waters and a stream of joy. Sometimes they are the best words the heart can speak."

My tears were indeed healing waters. The emotion that I had buried within me was finally coming out. Each time I grieved the void of not having a father, I found myself moving toward healing. To be in touch with myself was to know the depth of my wound.

I have learned that it's essential to perform a careful analysis of our emotions and to be introspective if we want to truly forgive the person who has harmed us. These actions help us to live healthier lives as individuals and to fully forgive our abusers. Not only do we learn about ourselves and some of our insecurities and triggers; we also become more aware of the depth of the wound that the person has caused.

To fully forgive we must be fully aware of the pain that the perpetrator caused.

To move forward, we must first be aware of our inner havoc and angst.

Most of the time, that's easier said than done.

5

Death and Resurrection

A Spiritual Take on Feeling

"For if we have been united with him in a death like his,
we will certainly also be united with him in a resurrection
like his."
Romans 6:5

"I have been crucified with Christ and I no longer live, but
Christ lives in me."
Galatians 2:20

"Very truly I tell you, unless a kernel of wheat falls to the
ground and dies, it remains only a single seed. But if it dies, it
produces many seeds. Anyone who loves their life will lose it,
while anyone who hates their life in this world will keep it for
eternal life."
John 12:24-25

Throughout Part I, titled "Feel the Pain," we slowly moved toward an awareness of our emotions and an exploration of their depths. In my own life, I learned that emotions can be insights—gateways—into reality (Chapter 1), that it is okay to feel confusing and disruptive things within myself (Chapter 2), that anger and hatred are okay but must be moved through and managed (Chapter 3), and that beneath anger is usually some form of sadness or grief that must be carefully evaluated and fully experienced (Chapter 4).

Throughout the Bible, a raw display of emotions unfolds—both on God's end and through the people who interact with him. In the Psalms, for example, David expresses a wide spectrum of emotions—

from being deeply moved by God's love to being overcome by feelings of vengeance, longing to repay his enemies. Often times his writings are raw, dark, and primitive, threaded with anger (see Psalm 137). As I read passages like that, I'm reminded that maybe emotion is okay after all. And maybe expressing the emotion in a safe context—which for David was in writing—and "letting it out," so to speak, can help make sure that we don't act upon it.

I've heard it said that one of Christ's purposes in his life and ministry was to teach us what it means to be fully human. Being fully human entails emotions. For example, Christ displays anger and frustration when he flips over tables in the temple, as I mentioned earlier. And he displays intense sorrow and agony when he is about to meet his death and contemplates what he has to do; he prays, "Father, if you are willing, take this cup from me; yet not my will, but yours be done" (Luke 22:42) in the Garden of Gethsemane. And he prays, "My God, my God, why have you forsaken me?" (Matthew 27:46) in his dying moments on the Cross.

To this point, in an article titled "Emotions, God's Nature" in *Christianity Today*, G. Walter Hansen, New Testament professor at Fuller Theological Seminary, writes, "I am spellbound by the intensity of Jesus' emotions: not a twinge of pity, but heartbroken compassion; not a passing irritation, but terrifying anger; not a silent tear, but groans of anguish; not a weak smile, but ecstatic celebration. Jesus' emotions are like a mountain river, cascading with clear water."

Christ's ability to be in touch with his emotions led to profound action. His anger toward the religious leaders of the day paved the way for a new, more inclusive spirituality and faith to emerge. His sorrow in the Garden of Gethsemane where he sweat drops of blood and begged for God to take the cup from him led to an incomprehensible act of surrender. His doubt on the cross led to the greatest display of faith the world has ever known. His ability to express the darkness of his emotions helped others to see the divine light shining from within him. His brokenness led to blessing. His death led to resurrection. The loss he endured on a physical, mental, emotional, and even spiritual level led to victory. Jesus did not seem to suppress anything. He knew that in every emotion, his life and mission was unfolding.

∞

There is no resurrection without the crucifixion, no rebirth without death.

Disney's 2015 animated film *Inside Out* is a brilliant depiction of the importance of our emotions. The movie focuses on a little girl's personified emotions of Joy, Sadness, Fear, Disgust, and Anger as her family moves to a different city and she's thrown into emotional turmoil. Not only was the movie interesting to watch with my daughter, who was about the same age of the girl in the movie and whose emotions I have seen change and evolve over the years, but it was also interesting to watch as a man of faith. In the movie, which seemed to be grounded in neuroscience and psychology, every emotion serves a purpose in the little girl's grieving process. Most interestingly, the movie portrayed that one can't have joy without sadness and can't have sadness without joy. They are partners in healing. I thought it was a beautiful demonstration of the gospel—of how there is no resurrection without the crucifixion and no rebirth in our own lives without death.

It seems to me that churches are pretty good at focusing on the resurrection—the hope, the victory, the story of a savior who conquers sin and death. Especially in America, we love the idea of "winning." It is much more difficult, however, for us to sit in the gravity of the loss. The rejection and abuse that Jesus experienced. The depths of emotional agony he endured. The crucifixion he suffered. The three painful days of waiting where early Christians believed they'd never see their savior again. We like to get to the "good part"—the conclusion, the end of the story. But it's in the life of Jesus that we too learn how to live. His resurrection simply affirms, in a miraculous way, that how Christ lived is worth modeling.

In his article "The Hidden Hope in Lament," Christian psychologist Dan Allender writes, "Christians seldom sing in the minor key. We fear the somber; we seem to hold sorrow in low esteem. We seem predisposed to fear lament as a quick slide into doubt and despair, failing to see that doubt and despair are the dark soil that is necessary to grow confidence and joy."

Instead of lamenting and experiencing the depth of our emotions, we have created "quick fixes" and formulated well-packed theological answers to suffering. This had led to rampant suppression of emotions amongst believers. And no wonder the church continues to witness so many implosions amongst its leadership and its members. We all have doubts and frustrations built up within ourselves, but we keep sprinkling our problems with holy water. A little bit of hope. A little bit of love. A little bit of "God has a plan."

Allender continues, "To lament—that is to cry out to God with our doubts, our incriminations of him and others, to bring a complaint against him—is the context for surrender. Surrender—the turning of our heart over to him, asking for mercy, and receiving his terms for restoration—is impossible without battle. To put it simply, it is inconceivable to surrender to God unless there is a prior, declared war against him."

In feeling pain, we experience the depth of our laments. Suppressing our emotions only leads to a tension that will almost always make us snap when we are triggered. Suppression is like an infection that never allows emotional wounds to heal. How can we find peace if we ignore the depth of the injustice? We have to go through our own deaths to see life on the other side. You never know what you have until you reach the lowest of lows. As Psalm 30:5 (NLT) says, "Weeping may last through the night, but joy comes with the morning." The great challenge is to endure the night.

Similarly, lament is also essential in moving toward forgiveness. Without experiencing the range of the emotions associated with the trauma, without understanding the breadth of the wound, it is impossible to fully forgive the abuser for what he or she has done. How can we forgive if we do not understand?

"The temptation is to believe that our emotions indicate that there is something wrong with us, but the truth is that our emotions usually indicate that there is something wrong with our situation."

Our emotions can help us to better understand ourselves—both the pains and passions within us. During this process of self-discovery, we are welcomed onto a journey of God-discovery, where we discover the divine through ourselves, in the interior temple where God resides.

In 2016, I was asked to speak to a group of teenagers at a church summer camp. I shared with them some of the stories about my complicated relationship with my dad that are included in these pages, and I challenged them to write down the name of someone in their life who they had not yet forgiven.

When the kids wrote down the names of people who had harmed them or mistreated them, it was like God poked a hole in their souls that relieved all the tension that had been building within them. Lots of tears. Lots of hugs. But in that brokenness, they realized that they were all *one*—that they could all unite around the things inside themselves that they did not understand. And they realized that it was okay to express themselves—to show their emotion—because everyone was doing it.

I was reminded of how most kids are trained—either by their families or culture—to bottle up their emotions and hide what they are feeling so that they don't come across as "weak" or "emotional." There were so many moments with my dad that triggered emotions that I suppressed for this very reason.

The temptation is to believe that our emotions indicate that there is something wrong with us, but the truth is that our emotions usually indicate that there is something wrong with our situation. I wish I'd opened up more and shared my feelings more in my life. I wish I'd gone to more counseling. I wish I'd not been ashamed of how I felt. And I wish I'd had the courage of those kids when I was younger—to step into that vulnerable state and truly process what had happened in my life.

I did not fully feel the weight of the pain from not having a father until well into my adult life. And for most of my life, I wasn't sure if I'd ever be able to forgive my father for his absence and recklessness.

PART II
EVALUATING THE TRAUMA

"It takes time—lots of it—to feel, to grieve, to listen, to reflect, to be mindful of what is going on around us and in us, to live and not simply exist, and to love well."

Peter Scazzero, *Emotionally Healthy Spirituality*

6

Becoming a Man

The Importance of Evaluating

In the moments that mattered the most to me, Joe Romano either wasn't there at all, or he was drunk and I wished he wasn't there. The deep longing he created in me for presence was often met by absence. He was an occasional and disappointing presence in my life.

When I graduated from high school, the story was no different.

I know that for some people, graduating from high school isn't that big of a deal. (For my middle brother, Chris, high school was a cakewalk. He finished eighth overall in his class and was one of the top students in the school—and he did it effortlessly.) But for me, it *was* a big deal. I always struggled in school, and I had to work really hard to keep my grades up. The fact that I was going to graduate and was set to attend college the following year was a *really* big deal for me.

I think that Nana and Pa understood the significance of my achievement. Not only was I their first grandchild to graduate, but I had also seemed to pave the way and set the trend for my two younger brothers, proving that despite our traumatic home life, we could still go on to do great things individually. I was extremely proud of myself.

But something very large was missing on my graduation day: my father.

He was in rehab.

Though I was happy that he had gone to rehab for the first time, it hurt that he was not there for the crowning achievement of my high school career. As proud as I felt that day, Dad's absence—which was a reflection of his lifelong absence—hit me hard after the ceremony. The ever-present void I felt was very tangible and real.

After the graduation ceremony, I went to Ed's house for a celebration. Being with him and my friends was exactly what I needed. They understood my situation and the challenges I was facing with my dad. And I was able to commemorate an accomplishment with people who loved me and who were there for me.

By that time in my life, being let down by Dad was becoming a pattern. I was beginning to understand that I needed to lower my expectations for him—even during some of my most meaningful moments. I was also beginning to see that I needed to distance myself from him. It was a sad reality. My brothers came to this conclusion, too, and we each started calling our father "Joe" instead of "Dad."

Interestingly, my mother recently found a letter that my dad sent us from rehab one month after my graduation. In the letter, you can see that he is beginning to come to grips with the seriousness of his alcoholism, just as we were, too. Here is the first part of the letter:

> Dear Boys,
>
> I need to write this to you and really be sincere. We just saw a film concerning children of alcoholics. I want you boys to know that my disease is a family one. It doesn't mean that you will become a problem drinker, it just means that the risk is high that if you use, you could develop a problem. I know you probably are aware of this, but I feel it is my duty to remind you all. Your mother has done well to help you boys. All I can do is be an example to you that a person can recover from alcoholism.

∞

I'm not sure this "distancing" of myself from my father was a conscious decision, but somewhere deep down in my soul, I knew that I needed to get away. The fact that Cayuga Community College had such a good broadcasting school made it a perfect fit.

And so I attended Cayuga with Ed, who was also getting a broadcasting degree. We chose to room together and rented an off-campus apartment. My grandparents, being the generous people who they were, decided to help me with my rent. I think they knew how good it would be for me to get away from Ravena.

They were right.

Going away was vital for my health and growth as a man.

Cayuga felt like freedom. I was free from Joe. Free from my peers' perceptions of my family. Free from any social label that had been tied to me. It was like being given an opportunity to start all over—a second chance at my life far away from all the memories that seemed to pull me down. Far away from the angst, drama, and continual disappointment.

It felt like my world was opening up.

To begin, I *loved* broadcasting. I loved my classes. I loved working for the on-campus radio station. And for perhaps the first time in my life, I felt like I had found something that I was naturally good at. I began to dream about my future for the first time. I wanted to work in radio. More specifically, I wanted to work in sports media.

In Ravena, it'd felt like I was always too close to my dad's issues and the abuse to think about myself or pursue my own dreams. Having the freedom to pursue the growing desires deep within me was a game-changer.

Ed and I really had a good time our freshman year. We would often go on weekend road-trips, and every Monday night during the fall and winter, we would go to a local restaurant and eat an ungodly amount of ten-cent wings while watching Monday Night Football. We always had a lot of fun.

Socially, I found myself gaining a lot of confidence. I went on a number of dates while at Cayuga, and my apartment, as I mentioned, ironically became *the* place for parties.

I quickly learned while off on my own that there were a lot of basic things—"street smarts" stuff—that I had not learned because the practicality had gotten lost in my chaotic childhood, lost to my father's alcoholism.

Once, for example, I remember getting rear-ended, getting out of my car to make sure the person was okay, and then—without even exchanging insurance information or checking my bumper—getting back into my car and driving away. Another time, when my roommates and I first moved into our apartment, I remember ignorantly eating and drinking anything that was in the refrigerator or in our cabinets— even stuff that didn't belong to me. Like the car accident, I didn't think anything about it. Then one morning I woke up to see that all the food and drinks were labeled with their names. That's when I finally understood. But there was a disconnect within me when it came to very practical things.

Being away at college allowed me to learn these things. My second year at Cayuga, people started saying to me, "You're different, Jay." I had matured.

Overall, my two years at Cayuga helped me to become a more confident, whole, and well-rounded person. Free from the abuse stemming from Dad's alcoholism, I finally felt able to discover my own passions—for the first time in my life. Instead of constantly reacting to my father's deplorable actions, I became proactive in my own life. Instead of feeling trapped in the madness of the abuse, I found a joy and contentment within myself. Instead of always being pulled backwards into a toxic situation that inevitably hurt me and ruined my day, I began moving forward.

There was distance between me and the abuser. It created space for personal growth to take place. I began to dream. I began to have more fun than I'd ever had in my life. I began to find joy. And I began making decisions *for myself* because I was less bound to my dad.

∞

Boundaries free you to evaluate your hurt and enter into your own journey.

My decision to move away, much like the instance when I fled into the bathroom in my youth and locked the door, was something that I naturally felt inclined to do. I think this natural inclination of having to get away was inspired by my mother. She is a strong woman—confident in herself and unwilling to remain in any situation where she is being mistreated.

Just as she planted a seed in my brothers and me to express our emotions by taking us to counseling, she also planted a seed in us to have the courage to create boundaries. When I was fifteen years old, for example, I witnessed an intense argument between Mom and our stepfather, Dennis. We were somewhat used to verbal spats between them, but this time, all of a sudden, Dennis shoved my mother to the ground. I was almost too shocked to feel angry. As verbally abusive as Joe was, he never laid a hand on me, my brothers, or my mother. Once Mom got back up on her feet and regained her composure, she screamed,

"Boys, get your stuff! We need to go!" We quickly packed our things, piled into Mom's car, and spent the night at a local motel. I remember watching the Super Bowl a few days later at Ed's house, where my family was staying to avoid Dennis, and thinking to myself, "Why am I not even allowed to be in my own house?"—a house that Mom had bought with her hard-earned money, no less. Another abusive man was intruding on our happiness.

Within the next eighteen months, Mom had filed for divorce. It was all a horrible situation—something no son should have to see. But Mom's ability to protect herself—to protect us and put up a firm boundary—always stuck with me.

Now I can see that this "distancing" from abusive people is essential in order to live a healthy life and to grow and mature. When I was in college, the distance between my father and me was the proverbial door between us. And, just like when I was younger—huddled on the floor of that bathroom behind a locked door so that I could scream bloody-murder—getting away from my father was absolutely necessary.

One of my favorite movies is the 1994 drama *When a Man Loves a Woman*, starring Meg Ryan (who plays Alice Green) and Andy Garcia (who plays Alice's husband, Michael). I think the movie has always resonated with me because it unfolds in the throes of Alice's alcoholism. In the movie, Michael eventually makes the decision to put up a boundary to protect their children and himself. Every time I watch this movie, it tears me to pieces. It is a gripping story of an American family that is plagued by a parent's alcoholism. It shows the helplessness, emotions, and surrender that both Alice and Michael had to experience to move toward healing. It was difficult for Michael to distance himself and his children from the love of his life, but he had no choice. That has always stuck with me.

"The abusers in our lives—those who constantly tear us down and hurt us—can do a lot of horrible things, things that we can't control. But we should never be deterred from pursuing our own passions and our dreams."

It can be difficult to break free from the grip of abusive people because they are often people we love—our family, friends, and significant others. People who we are attached to. People who we think that we can fix or heal. But we cannot forget to love and heal ourselves in the process. The abusers in our lives—those who constantly tear us down and hurt us—can do a lot of horrible things, things that we can't control. But we should never be deterred from pursuing our own passions and our dreams. We should never stop making decisions that reflect our love for ourselves and our own value as we live the precious, beautiful lives that God has blessed us with. And we can demonstrate that we love both ourselves and our abusers by putting up boundaries.

In his book *Boundaries*, author Henry Cloud writes, "Boundaries define us. They define what is me and what is not me. A boundary shows me where I end and someone else begins, leading me to a sense of ownership. Knowing what I am to own and take responsibility for gives me freedom. Taking responsibility for my life opens up many different options."

Putting up boundaries also helps us move toward peace and forgiveness. If we remain in an abusive relationship with no boundaries, it is difficult to move toward forgiveness. If we never remove ourselves from the hurt, there's no space to process the pain. Even scarier, we never move toward peace, because the abuse becomes our reality.

Though my going off to school three hours away was hardly a conscious move toward forgiveness for me, what it represents is relevant. Ultimately, my moving away created a geographical boundary and better positioned me to find myself and become my own person—no longer attached to the toxicity, negativity, and confusion that had constantly pulled me down throughout my childhood and my formative years in middle school and high school.

We need to remove ourselves from abusive situations if we hope to become who we are meant to be. If we struggle or fail to remove ourselves from abusive situations, then maybe we don't see ourselves the way God sees us, maybe we don't have a very high regard for our lives, and maybe, just maybe, we don't truly love ourselves.

7

Those Dreaded Phone Calls

Developing Boundaries to Keep Others Out

After a boundary is created, the abuser—or the person who is being kept out—will often try to weasel his or her way back into your world, often through manipulation. Sometimes this manipulation is intentional; other times it's what the person does when he or she feels like something has been taken away.

It was no different with Dad. His attempts to break back into my world often came through his routine phone calls. He used his phone to try and reel me back into the abuse. The most difficult thing about Dad's drunken calls was that he would berate me. He would try to guilt-trip me about never coming home and would often go on cursing tirades about me and my brothers, littered with name calling and other kinds of verbal abuse. Although he was drunk, it was still difficult to hear my own father say such horrible things about me.

Although I don't have many memories of Dad calling me my first year at Cayuga—perhaps because he was in rehab or maybe because I was so absorbed in my life there—his phone calls in his drunken stupors escalated my second year of college.

And I didn't like it.

I had realized by that point that I liked my space. I liked my life without his negative influence. Though I might not have consciously created the boundary between us by going off to Cayuga, I had caught a glimpse of how much healthier and happier I was when there was space between us. I started realizing that it was up to me to maintain that space if I cared about my own health.

When Dad called me while he was drunk, I would often say to him, "Dad, I can tell that you are drinking again; please don't call me while you're drunk," and then I would hang up the phone. But he hardly ever listened. He'd always keep calling me.

When he realized that I was sticking to my boundaries—always hanging up the phone if he was drunk—he began trying different tactics to reel me in. Again, I'm not sure if he realized he was doing this—he was drunk, after all—but it's what many abusers naturally do when they are confronted with boundaries.

∞

It was after nine o'clock in the evening in February of 1993 when the phone started to ring. I had class early the next morning, and I knew it could only be one person: my dad.

I picked up the phone and heard an automated voice on the other end: "You have received a collect call from: *Jay, don't hang up; it's your dad.* Press '1' to accept the call. Press '2' to decline the call."

It was always discouraging to receive collect calls from Dad because it meant that his alcoholism had spiraled out of control and that he was in rehab or in trouble. It would also put us in a tough spot because if we declined the call, Dad would know that we had picked up and decided to decline.

That night, I accepted the call. I heard a very broken, sad person on the other end. Dad bluntly said to me, "Jay, I just can't take it anymore; I think I am going to kill myself."

I confronted him and asked him why he was sharing this news with me. I wondered: Was it for attention? For sympathy? To try to get me to come home? Was this another scheme of his?

I eventually dismissed the comment, figuring he was just trying to get attention, and quickly wrapped up the call. Then I went to bed.

As I lay in bed, I remember thinking to myself, *What if he actually does it?*

And then a very dark thought came to my mind, *Well, that's one less thing I'd have to worry about.*

That was a horrible, selfish thing to think about my own father, but it was truly how I felt at the time, as a nineteen-year-old kid. I think the fact that my mind even went this direction is a reflection of how discouraged I was. It felt like I was in a never-ending free fall. I had heard him utter some unspeakable things to me out of anger before, but never had I heard him say something so drastic.

He probably wanted me to do some action to show I loved him. But the best way I could show this love toward him was by establishing boundaries. Each time he called me when he was drunk, my deepest desire was to immediately hop in my car, find him, and do everything I could to heal him. That's how much I cared about him. I wanted to help, to *force* him to sober up. But the battle wasn't mine to fight; it was between him and God. If he really wanted to conquer his alcoholism, then he needed to establish a support team and accountability. And his support team *couldn't* be his family. His sons were too deeply connected to the trauma.

Though my dad might not have understood, the best way for me to show him how much I cared about him and loved him often unfortunately meant telling him no—that I would not cave to his desperate pleas for attention. If I started comforting him every time he told me something drastic, he probably would have started sharing heavy and desperate things with me to reengage me in his life and situation.

Looking back on that suicide call, I wish I had immediately called my mom or the cops after Dad threatened to kill himself, because the truth is that I would have felt extremely guilty had something actually happened to him. But I was young, stunned, and didn't know what to do. I just knew I couldn't reengage myself in his fight.

So I shrugged off the call as him being dramatic in his drunkenness. The next morning I called my mom, wanting to make sure that nothing had happened. She said that she hadn't heard anything and assumed that he was fine.

I was relieved but was also reminded that the situation was only worsening and that his attempts to manipulate me and my brothers were becoming more severe. That meant only one thing: that we had to build up the boundary walls even higher to protect ourselves as much as possible from retraumatization.

Another time, Dad called and asked if he could borrow some money from me. Imagine that: your own father calling to ask you for money because he spent his paycheck on booze. "Dad," I told him, "I'm a nineteen-year-old college sophomore; I don't have any money."

The conversation was completely absurd to me. It was one of many calls that I placed in the "baffling" category of my memory. I didn't have money. I was one of three people living in a two-bedroom apartment. Actually, I was living in a utility closet, sleeping on an uncomfortable twenty-five-dollar bed, to save money on rent. I was on a tight budget—taking out loans and working at the radio station and paying rent—and he was a grown man with a teaching job living in his parents' house. And he asked *me* for money. I remember thinking to myself, *Is it that bad?* That's a heck of a mess—and a heck of a burden to put on your son.

Looking back, I think that Dad truly thought, in his warped mind, that I would feel sorry for him that he had spent all his money. I began realizing that when he was drunk, he victimized himself—thinking a "woe is me" attitude could rope those he loved back into his life. He acted like a kid, and his alcoholism *never* allowed him to grow up and mature. His lack of control in his own life led him to try to manipulate and control the people he loved the most.

Sometimes he'd call me and ask me to come pick him up because he was drunk. He was just trying to get my attention. I would tell him no. But I sometimes felt guilty not going to get him or refusing to send him any money. I thought: *What if something happens to him? What if he's in danger? But if I don't say no, when will he stop?* Whenever I denied his requests, he usually responded with anger and rage. But I *had* to take the risk of him yelling at me to stay in control of the situation—to protect myself.

He tried to take advantage of the guilt I felt, too. Sometimes he'd say, "It's your fault that I drink."

"Had you just picked me up…"

"Had you just given me that money…"

It's honestly easier to say yes to an abuser, because then the problem seems to go away and you don't have to tell them no and listen to their angry responses. But the reality is that the problem doesn't go away; you merely enable the abuser. Sometimes the toughest love is the love you have to leave behind. And that means leaving behind the guilt, too. Because the truth is that the situation is *not* your fault—and it never was. Christian rock-band MercyMe has a wonderful song called "Dear Younger Me" with this beautiful line: "Dear younger me / It's not your fault / You were never meant to carry this beyond the Cross." MercyMe lead singer Bart Millard *also* had an abusive, alcoholic father.

That song—and particularly that line—has always stuck with me.

Realizing that the situation was not my fault helped me to step into a place of empowerment. And when Joe started calling our landline phone at our college apartment in the middle of the night, I knew that it was time to take action. I decided to write him a letter, asking him to stop calling me. This was the first time I'd ever expressed any desire to cut off communication with him. My youngest brother Damian also did this at one point, and he went two years without talking to Joe. Although my roommates understood my situation, it was still embarrassing when Dad's calls woke them up and I had to explain to them that my own father was drunk calling me again.

My dad's actions and decisions had already tainted and scarred many areas of my life, and I was determined not to let him negatively affect my college experience, too. My world was beginning to open up, and I wasn't going to let my dad pull me back into his.

As author Henry Cloud says in his book *Boundaries*, "Boundaries are a way to describe our spheres of responsibility: what we are and are not responsible for."

∞

In the summer of 1998, I received another memorable call from Dad. I had been dating Dawn for about a year, and on that evening, we were hanging out. When I picked up the phone, I could hear Dad crying on the other end of the line. This was very, very rare. It also seemed like he was sober. After all, he didn't usually get sad when he was drunk; he got angry. *What's going on?*

"Dad, what's wrong?" I asked.

He proceeded to go on a long, broken spiel about his ex-wife, Patty, the woman from his second marriage who he deeply loved. Then he blurted out, "Jay, Patty is dead."

Though I hadn't talked to Patty in years, we *had* lived with her and my dad in my grandparents' house during my childhood, and I knew how much Dad loved and cared for her. It was strange to realize that my stepmom, someone who had positively impacted my life despite my father's alcoholism, had passed away. Patty had even come to my high school graduation while my Dad was away at rehab.

"That's terrible, Dad," I said. "I'm so, so sorry."

"Yeah, I got a call from someone," he continued. "She burned down in a house. Her house caught fire, and she died."

We talked for a little longer, and then he said goodbye. I called my brothers, and we processed the loss together on the phone.

About a week later, I received another call from Dad.

Again, he was sober.

"Jay, I need to tell you something," he said bluntly. "Patty isn't dead. I made that story up."

I'm not sure what led him to make such a confession—he usually didn't have a single introspective bone in his body (many people who identify as victims don't)—but he confessed nonetheless.

Regardless, I was shocked that he'd made up such a horrific story. I became very angry and upset. I had already accepted she had died and had grieved her death with my brothers.

"You *lied* about Patty dying?" I exclaimed. "Why would you do that?"

I don't remember his response, but looking back, I think the story he fabricated was a cry for help. It was like he was saying, "Someone, please feel sorry for me; I don't feel like I can defeat this disease."

People didn't understand his alcoholism, including myself. People didn't understand that it was a disease. I used to hate it when he called it a "disease," because it always sounded to me like he was victimizing himself and not taking responsibility for his actions. And people didn't feel sorry for him or empathize with him because they didn't understand what he was going through. So he fabricated a story that would get people to feel sorry for him.

It took me a long time to trust him after that. I wondered, *What can I believe? What's true?* His manipulative tactics got more and more twisted and diabolical. Just like when I was living on my own at college and Dad tried to guilt-trip me to give him money or come home, Dad creating the story about Patty was another attempt to get me reengaged in his struggle.

But it was just one more reason to stick to my boundaries.

∞

Creating boundaries keeps a toxic person and his or her manipulative and controlling tactics out of your space so that you can live a healthy life.

When boundaries are established, the most natural thing for a boundary-less person to do is to break through those boundaries. But this is where boundaries become more important than ever. As difficult as it is to establish boundaries at the start, what's even more difficult—in my experience—is to maintain them and to keep building the walls higher if needed. It's especially difficult for victims to be empowered and to create boundaries because they have been told for so long, through the abuse, that they are not important.

Henry Could reiterates these ideas in *Boundaries*. He writes, "If you are a loving person, it will break your heart to say no to someone you love who is in need. But there are limits to what you can and can't give; you need to say no appropriately....These are the instances in which your broken heart wants to give, but you would burn out if you did."

"We need to better understand our pain if we hope to better understand ourselves. Boundaries can help us do that."

As difficult as establishing boundaries can be, my boundaries helped me to elevate my own mental and emotional health. I believe that creating boundaries can be done while being graceful and nonjudgmental to the abuser. I wasn't always the best at this. I wish I had been able to empathize with my dad's situation more without becoming reengaged. But it was difficult for me—especially when I had yet to fully deal with the trauma from my childhood.

To fully evaluate past trauma, the victim needs to first create distance between himself or herself and the abuser—and then must maintain this distance as the perpetrator tries to intrude and invade.

Moving to Cayuga gave me the space I needed to find myself. But it's important to note that finding ourselves also entails exploring our childhoods and our past wounds, since pain is a part of our reality and a part of why we are who we are today. If we never find the space to do that, we will most likely venture through life reacting to the things that repuncture our wound. We need to better understand our pain if we hope to better understand ourselves. Boundaries can help us do that.

When we stick to our boundaries, we create healthy spaces for ourselves. This can help us to discover who we really are, to find our true selves, and to perhaps draw closer to God in the process. As Saint Augustine writes in *Confessions*, "How can you draw close to God when you are far from your own self?"

When we don't establish boundaries, it is easier to lose ourselves, to forget who we really are: children of God.

8

The Most Important Day of My Life

Developing Boundaries to Keep Your Heart
and Mind In

Boundaries are not only meant to keep toxic people *out*; they're also meant to keep your own heart and mind *in*.

You should be aware of both your abuser's intentions *and* your own tendencies. This is important because, for most who have been betrayed by someone they love, it's easy for the victim's heart and mind to become reengaged, either directly or indirectly, with the abuser.

I had to guard my own heart and mind throughout my life in order to minimize retraumatization and to prevent myself from going into a reactive state that was connected to past trauma. There's no better example of this in my life than my wedding day…

I was twenty-three years old when I first met Dawn. I had just completed my bachelor's degree at the State University of New York at New Paltz, had just gotten out of a long-term relationship, and had just gone to therapy for the first time since my childhood. In high school and college, it was easy for me to bury myself in my schoolwork, extracurricular activities, and friends, but my shame and insecurity began to emerge more as I stepped into adulthood.

Though the story of how Dawn and I met is kind of embarrassing, I think it illustrates how unconfident I was at the time, how hesitant I was to even entertain the thought of welcoming someone into my life in such a vulnerable state, how out-of-touch I was with the dating scene, and how willing Dawn was through it all to meet me right where I was.

My mom set me up. Yep, that's right. I was very much against the idea and resisted for as long as I could, constantly telling Mom that I was fine and didn't want to meet Dawn. But Mom persisted and wouldn't leave either of us alone until we agreed to go on a date.

77

Unfortunately, it got worse. On our first date, I made the dire mistake of asking Dawn if she wanted to "go Dutch"—you know, split the check. In writing a book on forgiveness, I have to say I'm thankful that she let that one slide. That whole lack of "street smarts" thing again. But Dawn was just amazing in walking with me through it all.

After that, the rest is history. We had a connection, the strongest I had ever experienced, and we fell in love.

When we began planning our wedding, the looming question immediately became: If we have alcohol at our wedding reception, should we invite Joe Romano?

By this point in my mid-twenties, Dad's alcoholism had only worsened. He was in and out of rehab, had gotten two DWIs, and had lost his teaching job. His situation was crazy and terrible. This was also around this time that he qualified to collect disability checks because of his alcoholism. Now not only did he always have Nana and Pa's house to return to—a place for him to sleep—but he also received a good-sized monthly paycheck, which he often immediately cashed and took straight to the liquor store or the bar.

Would he ever hit rock bottom?

Protecting my own heart and mind became even more important during this time in my twenties, as I pursued my radio dreams and met the love of my life.

This is why it is important to establish boundaries with toxic people early on in your life if possible. You don't want the abuser to invade other areas of your life—your deepest dreams and closest relationships—as you grow older.

I think my brothers and I all hoped that our attitudes toward our father would help him hit rock bottom, which is another benefit to boundaries: they can help the abuser open his or her eyes to the simple truth that something needs to change if he or she wants the relationships back that matter the most.

Unfortunately, my dad's cycle of alcoholism only continued: a short span of sobriety would give us false hope, and then he'd drastically relapse—including drunken calls and unbridled rage—and he'd end up back in rehab.

Would things ever change?

As Dawn and I planned our wedding, I ran through all the possible scenarios of inviting my father: If we didn't have alcohol at our wedding, I'd worry the entire day that he would bring alcohol into the reception, just as I had seen him do at other places. And if we did have alcohol, I'd worry that he'd lose control.

In the end, we decided that we *would* have alcohol at our reception, just like most Catholic weddings in the northeast at the time, so the answer to whether or not we should invite my father seemed to be clear: no. But at one point, I actually defied all logic and concluded in my mind that I would *still* invite him. He was my dad, after all, and I wanted him there—more than anything. Especially considering all the important events in my life he had missed. But unlike the graduations he'd missed, my wedding was something I *could* control. That's why I wrestled so much with it.

A couple months before the wedding, however, a phone call pushed me over the edge. "By calling me while drunk, you just answered my question," I told him. I decided not to invite him to my own wedding. I just couldn't take the risk of him ruining the best day of my life.

You could say that choosing not to invite Dad was my own way of guarding my heart and my mind. I set boundaries to protect myself from becoming reengaged or distracted on the best day of my life. And as tough as it was to do, I'm thankful I did it. It positioned me to be present for the person who mattered most that day: Dawn.

We got married on a beautiful, fall, fifty-five-degree day in a Catholic cathedral in Colonie, New York. When I saw those double doors open and Dawn appear in her beautiful, white dress, it felt like my heart was going to beat out of my chest. It took everything within me just to hold it together. Part of me hoped that my mother would stand up and ask me another random question like she'd done at Nana's and Pa's fiftieth wedding anniversary to distract me from everything that I was feeling. I was a wreck!

Turns out, I held it together—until the reception, that is.

During our first dance, which happened to be to Shania Twain's "From This Moment On" with Bryan White, I broke down and began to sob on Dawn's shoulder. Even though I'm not a crier, I couldn't keep it together. I was always most emotional when I had to confront my family and my broken past.

As I danced with Dawn, I thought about how I was stepping into a brand new life. I had found someone who I loved with everything within me, someone who I wanted to spend the rest of my life with. And not only that, but with Dawn, I had an opportunity to do things the right way. I had an opportunity to make a marriage last. I had an opportunity to raise kids the right way—without alcohol or abuse and with love, compassion, peace, and understanding. I couldn't *wait* to be a father.

I even thought about my brothers as I danced with Dawn. Each of us wanted to break the chain of addiction in the Romano family. Each of us wanted to love and serve our families the way Dad never did. My wedding day was the ultimate culmination of everything that had happened before in my life—all that had been overcome. It also gave me hope that a new season was beginning, a new cycle in the Romano family, a new way of life that got back to the way that Nana and Pa lived. The fact that I was even in a position to get married to such a lovely, mature woman after all I'd been through felt like a miracle. While crying on Dawn's shoulder, I eventually turned to the crowd and yelled hysterically, "I'm such a mess!" which helped to break the ice.

The mother-and-son dance, which was to Chicago's "You're the Inspiration," was an emotional one, too. I'm Mom's firstborn. Not only that, but my personality is most similar to hers: sensitive and emotional.

Mom had seen me go through my trials with Dad, in school, and in relationships. She was my rock. I once wrote an essay about her because she was the most important person in my life. And now she was letting me go.

Later on in the reception, while I was sitting at a gigantic table with the rest of our wedding party, a woman who worked at the venue approached me and said, "Mr. Romano, you have a phone call." I looked at Dawn and gave her a confused shrug.

"Do you know who it is?" I asked.

"Yeah, it's your dad," she said.

An immediate bolt of anger came over me. I wanted to lash out. I wanted to take the phone call and chew him out. How dare he call me on my wedding day when he knew how much hearing from him—especially if he was drunk—would hurt me? And how did he even know where the reception was? None of my family would have told him. Did he call every reception hall in the Colonie/Albany area? There he was again, pushing my boundaries.

But then I took a few deep breaths, calmed down, and said to the woman, "I don't want to talk to him."

"I'll let him know that you aren't available," she replied.

∞

Creating boundaries keeps your own heart and mind in your space so that you can live a healthy life.

It was tempting to invite Dad to my wedding. And it was just as tempting to pick up the phone when he called me at my wedding. But I said no to both temptations in order to protect my heart and mind—not only for myself but also for Dawn. Not inviting him to my wedding, as difficult as it was, kept Dad *out*. And choosing not to answer his phone call at the reception, as difficult as that was, kept my heart and my mind *in*.

Maybe you're struggling with an ex-spouse who keeps intruding upon your life, making you wonder if you should get a new phone number. Or maybe it's an old friend or significant other who you need to block on social media because seeing their posts sends your heart and mind into a furious downward spiral of pain and memories. Maybe you have a spiritually abusive pastor or a congregation who judges you, making you question if you should switch churches. Maybe you need to go to therapy to help you navigate through your emotions. Maybe you need an accountability partner who checks on you daily to make sure that you haven't taken the bait of a manipulator who is trying to get you reengaged in an abusive situation.

Sometimes we can't control what an abuser or boundary-less person does to us. What we can control is what we allow to go out of ourselves. We all have power over the energy we choose to give to a situation.

Ultimately, our desire (or lack of desire) to guard our hearts and our minds from toxicity or abuse is a reflection of how we view ourselves. If we continue to gravitate toward abuse, then perhaps we do not have the self-worth that we should—or maybe we have become codependent, gripped by the fear of what our lives might look like without the person who is abusing us. That's not to say that our love for that person is not real. But it could also reveal to us that our love for ourselves is not as real or deep as it should be.

> "Ultimately, our desire (or lack of desire) to guard our hearts and our minds from toxicity or abuse is a reflection of how we view ourselves. If we continue to gravitate toward abuse, then perhaps we do not have the self-worth that we should."

Overall, it's difficult to move toward resolve and forgiveness if you do not understand the depth of your worth. In the Bible, Jesus says to love your neighbor as yourself, which might sometimes entail forgiving your neighbor, but it also implies that you need to love yourself. Many who are caught in abusive situations demonstrate that they do not truly love themselves through their inability to remove themselves from a situation and put up boundaries.

Some scholars have suggested that when Jesus says in his famous Sermon on the Mount to "turn the other cheek," he was actually presenting an alternative, non-dualistic way of seeing and approaching situations in which someone treats you as one who is "less than." Authors Glen Stassen and David Gushee explain in *Kingdom Ethics* that in its cultural context, being struck on the right cheek with the back of the right hand was an insult, and "to turn the other cheek was to surprise the insulter, saying, nonviolently, 'you are treating me as an unequal, but I need to be treated as an equal.'" And Jesus perhaps makes this profound political statement because he recognizes everyone's inherent worth—that there is "neither Jew nor Gentile, neither slave nor free, nor is there male and female," for all are "one in Christ Jesus," as Paul writes in Galatians 3:28. So in this context, in order to turn the other cheek, the abused must first understand their worth—their equality with their oppressor.

You are worthy. You matter. Your voice matters.

Protecting your heart and mind births courage and confidence because you are taking control of your life. Boundaries are a way for you to take intentional steps toward wholeness. They create space for you to more fully understand yourself.

We honor God through how we honor ourselves. Our view of God is a reflection of how we view ourselves. And the reality is that each of us has temptations in our lives from which we need to guard our hearts and minds. The lengths we go to guard our hearts and minds from things that harm us reveal how we view ourselves.

9

Letting Down Your Own Dad

Allowing Safe People to Enter Into Your Pain

One of the most challenging things in life is letting others into our deepest pains. It requires vulnerability, transparency, willingness to be weak, and acceptance that our wounds are a part of who we are and are vital aspects of our journeys.

When we let others into these fragile areas of our lives, as scary and vulnerable as this might be, we can better evaluate and assess the trauma of our pasts. We can find perspective in outside sources. Others empower us and walk with us as we continue on our journeys of healing. It is never *all* up to us—though we often think that it is. When we let others in, we find both rest and strength in our community of supporters. This is where genuine friendship and transformation occur: in vulnerability and transparency.

Letting my wife Dawn into this dark area of my life was difficult.

I've had a deep sense of shame about my dad for as long as I can remember. I never liked when my friends interacted with him, and I certainly never wanted to introduce my girlfriends to him. When I dated my first girlfriend in my early teen years, we hardly ever hung out at my house—I always went to her house. In middle school, I was usually embarrassed or afraid to have my friends over to my grand-parents' house if my dad was going to be around. Many of my friends looked up to their fathers and had dads who were intricately involved in their lives—coaching our sports teams and things like that—but my dad was a deep source of embarrassment for me. A couple of times, I remember him stumbling out into the yard as my friends and I were playing backyard football and, in slurred words, offering to play full-time quarterback. "Go back inside, Dad," I would say.

Of course, these demonstrations unfolded on a more public scale as

I got older. But I was always proverbially saying, "Go back inside, Dad; you're embarrassing yourself and your family."

My senior year of high school, as my basketball season unfolded, I asked my dad not to come to my basketball games anymore because he would show up drunk and yell throughout the whole game. Even after asking him not to show up, there was more than one occasion where I'd look up and see him in the gym. That really irked me. It was embarrassing. I wanted to hide him from my friends, teammates, and the community.

When I fell in love with Dawn, I wanted to hide my dad from her, too. Though I knew that I could never shelter her entirely from the pain my dad had caused in my life, I wished that I could. I never wanted her to see anything related to my dad. I wished that I could protect her from ever having to see those insecurities of mine, from ever having to see my dad metaphorically stumble into my space and trigger within me a life's worth of pain. I never wanted her to see my shame.

To top it off, Dawn came from a "normal" family. Her parents—strong Catholics who were committed to faith and family—were still together, whereas both of mine had been divorced twice. She had healthy conversations with her parents on the phone, whereas my dad would often curse me out and tell me how horrible of a son I was. And she could depend on her parents for anything, whereas I had to put up boundaries between me and my dad. When we were dating, there was sometimes an overwhelming sense of, "Why would she want to be with someone like *me*? Would she really want to marry into a family like *mine*?"

Unworthiness. Shame. Brokenness.

Though I had told Dawn some stories about my father's alcoholism while we were dating, my situation became very real to her one spring day in 1999. It was about a year before we were married, and we were at Saint Peter's Hospital in Albany with my family to support Pa during his double knee replacement surgery. Pa was seventy-five years old at the time, and a major surgery at that age is always a concern. But the surgery went well, and Pa had his entire family by his side to support him that day in the hospital: Nana, Dad, my brothers, their significant others, Dawn, and me.

At one point, around lunch, Dad got up and said, "I'm going to get a sandwich. Do you all want anything?"

We told him that we were fine, and he left.

Within the hour, Dad returned—no sandwich—and was a completely different person. Normally my dad is a joyful and bubbly person, but instead of saying, "Hey guys! How's it going?" as he normally would, he simply mumbled in a low voice, "*Howyadoin?*"

Today I might have said, "How dare you show up drunk in front of your father when he needed you most?" But I was embarrassed and shocked in front of Dawn and instead said something to the effect of, "Dad, it might be a good idea if you left, and we are going to get going, too."

When we got back to the car, I lost it. I started yelling and venting to Dawn, "I can't believe he freaking did this! How could he be so mean and disrespectful after everything his dad has done for him?" I was overwhelmed with anger and sadness.

"This sucks," I eventually said. "I haven't experienced something like this before with someone who I love."

Similar feelings from past experiences resurfaced, like the time he got drunk before we were supposed to go to the Mets-Cardinals game or the time he missed my high school graduation or the time he was absent at Nana and Pa's fiftieth anniversary or all those times growing up when his drunken presence at our sporting events embarrassed us.

With my grandfather being the best man I've ever known, and with Dawn—my future wife—being forced to witness that dysfunction, my dad's actions struck an even deeper chord within me that day.

I couldn't help but wonder if Dawn really wanted to be with me. Did she really want to enter into the brokenness of my life?

My shame had resurfaced, and she saw it on full display.

∞

Years later I was hanging out at my house with my buddy Scott after church. It also happened to be on my dad's birthday. Scott has since become one of my closest friends but back in 2005, we were just getting to know each other. I hadn't told Scott about Dad yet, but at the time, my relationship with my father was in one of its most fragile states. By that point in my life, I had gotten pretty good at hiding my shame and the broken aspects of my life.

Anyway, Scott and I were sitting on the couch watching football when my home phone began to ring. I had caller identification and saw that it was my dad calling. I didn't pick up. He called again minutes later. Again, I didn't pick up. A few minutes later he called again, and this time he left a disturbing drunken message on my answering machine—a message that Scott heard.

"F*** you, Jason!" Joe screamed. "You and your brothers all know it's my birthday today, and none of you have called me. You are the worst f***ing son there is. I have the worst f***ing family. Oh, and f*** your Cowboys."

A sort of awkwardness hung in the silence of my living room. My shame, once more, had been exposed—this time to a new friend.

I had no choice but to explain the message. The vulgarity and intensity of the message wasn't something that I could simply sweep under the rug. And so I told Scott about my broken relationship with Dad and my lifelong struggle with anger, hatred, and forgiveness. It all led to a beautiful, redemptive conversation.

Turns out, Scott also had a complicated relationship with his father. I didn't know that about him. And suddenly we were able to relate to one another in an entirely different way—in an area that was very sensitive to each of us and an area that takes a broken, wounded person to truly understand. To this day, whenever I am struggling with something stemming from the void Dad had caused in my life, Scott is one of the first people I call.

∞

We think that we can hide our wounds from others, but we can't. In our relationships that are genuine, honest, and intimate—and don't we all ultimately want to be known and to be loved on a deep level?—our wounds and our shame will be revealed, either directly or indirectly.

Like most, I have struggled to share my deepest hurts with others. But I've learned that whenever I'm resisting something, there is a good chance that I am suppressing the thing I need the most.

It was scary for Dawn to see my family and me in that fragile, broken state in Pa's hospital room when my dad showed up drunk, and it was scary for Scott to hear the vulgar message that Joe left on my answering machine, yet it was good that they witnessed those situations. Dawn met me where I was just by being there for me and staying with me in that painful place. And Scott did the same. Dawn and Scott both demonstrated to me that they wanted to enter into the process *with* me. That's what best friends do, even when we think that our situation is too dark or too embarrassing or too shameful for anyone outside of ourselves.

And I felt more known and loved in the process.

∞

To sift through past pain or trauma, we have to be vulnerable and let others into our broken worlds.

In his book *Scary Close*, Donald Miller writes, "I don't mean to overstate what is yet unknown, but part of me believes when the story of earth is told, all that will be remembered is the truth we exchanged."

It was difficult for me to exchange the truths of my life with others outside of my brothers, particularly my wife Dawn. I hated that she glimpsed my deepest hurts, but it was inevitable. Our facades always break down. Our shame always seems to be revealed. What makes more sense is for us to accept that darkness is a part of our stories. In fact, it is often in the darkness—*in* the brokenness—where real transformation takes place. This is not only true for ourselves but also for others. When we share our brokenness, true connection unfolds. Author Brennan Manning writes in his book *The Ragamuffin Gospel*, "To live by grace means to acknowledge my whole life story, the light side and the dark. In admitting my shadow side I learn who I am and what God's grace means."

> "What makes more sense is for us to accept that darkness is a part of our stories. In fact, it is often in the darkness—in the brokenness—where real transformation takes place."

It took a long time for me to be willing to share the fragile aspects of my story. Four decades, to be exact. Just as I was afraid to let Dawn into that area of my life, I was also afraid to share it with others. Even when I became a follower of Jesus and started to go to church, I was hesitant to share my deepest wounds with my friends there. And even when I started to gain a significant following on Twitter because of my career in sports media and began posting Bible verses in an effort to encourage others, I was hesitant to share what was *really* going on in my life spiritually. Of course, in our well-connected society, there is such a thing as "oversharing," but I was on the opposite end of the spectrum. For a long time, I shied away from sharing anything vulnerable. I stuck to the whole "hope" aspect of faith—jumping to the resurrection instead of the painful life Jesus lived, as I mentioned in an earlier chapter.

Throughout my twenties and thirties, I would talk to my brothers about Joe's struggles and would sometimes talk to Dawn, but that was it. Even talking to God about Dad's alcoholism became monotonous. Just as I feared letting others in, I also began to doubt that God really wanted to enter that aspect of my life. It was too dark. Too hopeless. Too much of a lost cause.

Almost every day, I would pray to God, "Lord, help Dad to stop drinking," or "Help Dad to stay sober," but when I finished the prayer I would think to myself, "That's not gonna happen."

Slowly, however, over the years, I began to let others in. I opened up to two good friends at church about my dad's alcoholism, and it turns out, they both had issues with their fathers. We bonded over our brokenness. I even began to sometimes post things on social media, requesting prayers about my dad's struggles. I was shocked how much encouragement I received from people who I didn't even know. Others connected with me about some of their own family members' addictions simply because I opened up about mine. I realized that I had a community of prayer.

Surrounding myself with others, both physically and virtually, was invaluable to me. I began to evaluate the pain in different ways and learn from others' journeys of forgiveness. I began to confront the wound head-on—not because I was strong, but because I had an army of people who knew me and loved standing beside and behind me. It was a beautiful thing. And it was key to processing my pain, and therefore moving toward peace and forgiveness.

Best of all, when I opened up, others did as well. My willingness to share my brokenness created a safe space for others to share theirs. I was starting to discover that, yes, it sucked to go through what I went through, but there was a community of others going through the same thing. And through that, it helped me to better process my pain and approach the idea of healing, and maybe even some day, forgiveness.

At the end of 2014, I wrote a blog called "I Forgive You, Dad" that reached a large amount of people through the power of the Internet. And in 2015, I delivered a sermon about my lifelong struggle with my father for the first time. Now I am writing a book about my journey. And while I was working on this book, I left my job in sports media with the hopes of preaching more about my journey.

Though I didn't realize it at the time, when Dawn chose to enter my life in my mid-twenties despite the darkness she saw from my past, it helped open me up to let others, like Scott, into my struggles later in my life. And each time I let someone into that fragile, vulnerable place in my life, I began to see the light at the end of a long, long tunnel. Having others in my life who wanted to understand my situation helped me to better evaluate the pain and move through the grief.

10

Boxes in the Attic

A Spiritual Take on Evaluating

"In the beginning was the Word, and the Word was with God, and the Word was God. He was with God in the beginning. Through him all things were made; without him nothing was made that has been made. In him was life, and that life was the light of all mankind... The Word became flesh and made his dwelling among us. We have seen his glory, the glory of the one and only Son, who came from the Father, full of grace and truth."
John 1:1-4; 14

"Jesus knew that the Father had put all things under his power, and that he had come from God and was returning to God; so he got up from the meal, took off his outer clothing, and wrapped a towel around his waist. After that, he poured water into a basin and began to wash his disciples' feet, drying them with the towel that was wrapped around him."
John 13:3-5

In our Connecticut home is an attic that, like most attics, is jam-packed with boxes. Some of the boxes are stuffed with belongings from our family's past; some have seasonal decorations like Christmas lights or Easter baskets; and some are simply filled with junk that would probably be better off in the garbage.

Each time I go up in the attic to get something, which is about two or three times a year, I'm surprised to see all the stuff that I have forgotten about. Boxes of memories that haven't been opened in decades, covered with dust and cobwebs. Boxes of decorations that make me think of holidays past. Boxes of junk that I am just too lazy to sift through and throw away.

While I'm up there, I usually have a nagging feeling that there's work that needs to be done. But then I think about how long the task would take and how strenuous it would be. So I usually just get what I need and say to myself, "I'll clean this place up another time." The boxes remain. The dust thickens. The cobwebs become more intricate.

Now imagine that your soul—your heart and your mind—is an attic.

Inside our attics are boxes of repressed and suppressed memories—forgotten experiences, pains that still sit in our psyche and shape our actions, interactions from our childhoods stuffed in the deep recesses of our souls. Sometimes we are triggered by something and venture into that mysterious place, but the easiest thing to do when confronted with the mess—instead of evaluating our emotions and our pains—is to say, "I'll do that another time," and leave the attic in a hurry so that we can avoid confronting what we can't understand.

Though leaving boxes untouched in a physical attic might simply mean more dust and cobwebs, refusing to sift through and clean up our "soul attics" can produce long-term, destructive psychological effects. We will most likely go through life being reactive rather than proactive, always looking to fill the voids our insecurities left with pursuits that we think will fulfill us.

This section of the book is titled "Evaluating the Trauma" because in my experience, the easiest thing has been to treat my pain the same way I treat the boxes in my attic at home. Ignore it all. Press on. Leave the boxes in the corner to gather dust and cobwebs.

But once I gained the courage to feel my emotions, the next step in moving toward peace and forgiveness was to evaluate what had happened to me. This helped me to see how my wounds had shaped me so that I could better handle my insecurities and move toward health.

Even when I became a Christian in adulthood, I still managed to avoid opening those forlorn, terrifying boxes. I would proverbially venture up into the attic, notice the box, and flippantly pray a prayer that went like, "God, please deal with that box," and then I'd go back down the ladder.

Sticking to the same metaphor, the next time I went back up into the attic—usually whenever I got a call from my dad or whenever he relapsed or whenever something else happened related to his alcoholism—I'd see the same box there, mysteriously moved to the center of the attic. It was as if God was calling me to open it and sift through it. I might open a flap or two and peek inside, but then, terrified of what I saw, I would quickly close the flaps and kick the box into the corner. The next time I went back up into the attic, perhaps to retrieve something that wasn't even related to my dad's alcoholism, I might trip over the box, which again had magically moved, and then once again kick it away.

My point is that our deepest wounds are always resurfacing in mysterious ways. You may as well feel the pain and then carefully evaluate what is inside each box with your mind so that you no longer trip over them. After all, tripping over boxes can get really annoying. It's your attic, and they're your boxes, whether you asked for them or not. It's your journey, and your brokenness can be turned into a blessing for others.

Throughout Part II, titled "Evaluating the Trauma," we have moved toward creating a safe place where our emotions and our pasts can be carefully evaluated. In my own life, I learned that creating boundaries can create space for introspection and discovery to take place (Chapter 6), that they can keep toxic and abusive people *off* your property (Chapter 7), that they can keep our hearts and minds *on* our own property (Chapter 8), and that they can make room for healthy people to enter into our struggles with us (Chapter 9). Allowing ourselves to feel (Part I) is one thing, but creating space to evaluate what God might be telling us about reality through our emotions (Part II) is another. Whereas feeling is natural, journeying inward to evaluate our interior lives requires a lot of hard work.

But I was not alone when I dared to open the boxes in my attic. God was with me. God was the one who magically moved the box to the middle of the attic. He was the one making me trip over the box each time I went up into the attic. And when I finally decided to open the box, he was there to walk with me through the trial. To strengthen me. To guide me.

In his book *Walking with God through Pain and Suffering*, pastor and theologian Timothy Keller nails it when he says, "Suffering can refine us rather than destroy us because God himself walks with us in the fire."

Maybe you are struggling with a box in your attic. Maybe you want to keep the box closed and taped up. Maybe you are afraid. I'm here to tell you: it's okay, and it's fine to not be okay. Opening that box will send you on the journey of a lifetime, but it has to be in your timing. It might be difficult, but you will find yourself slowly moving toward healing.

∽

When evaluating past trauma and pain, our suffering savior is there to guide us and enter into our wounds with us.

From my perspective, the most dominant message in the ministry of Jesus Christ was that God is *with* the broken, *with* the suffering, *with* the forgotten, *with* those who were alienated and on the outside of society and religion. Christ displayed through his life that God is one who gravitates toward the margins. He did this in multiple ways, whether it was through something as culturally taboo as chatting with a Samaritan woman and adulteress at a well (John 4), meeting with a tax collector (Luke 19), or uniting a group of misfit ragamuffins and making them his disciples.

And not only did he live this way—he taught this way, too. In Luke 15:1-7 (The Parable of the Lost Sheep), Jesus tells a story about how a shepherd (representing God) will leave his ninety-nine sheep to find the one who has gone astray. In Luke 15:8-10 (The Parable of the Lost Coin), Jesus tells a story about a woman (representing God) who has ten silver coins but loses one and searches the house to find it. And in Luke 15:11-32 (The Parable of the Lost Son), he tells a story about a father (representing God) who pursues both his rebellious son who is plagued by shame and his self-righteous son who is angered by how his brother is welcomed home with open arms. The underlying point in all three of these stories is that God cares deeply about the one who is lost or in pain or discouraged.

God meets us right where we are, and we feel his presence even more when we are in fragile, lost, or broken states.

I find all of this to be extremely encouraging because opening boxes entails an immense deal of suffering. It is scary. It is difficult. It is confusing. It is painful. But you can be comforted by the fact that the

God of the universe is one who cares deeply about your past hurt, your present pain, and your future journey inward. Even though it is perhaps the loneliest journey you could ever embark upon—filled with grieving and things that you cannot understand, you will not be abandoned by God. As I have been saying, there is joy at the bottom of the pain.

> *"It is scary. It is difficult. It is confusing. It is painful. But you can be comforted by the fact that the God of the universe is one who cares deeply about your past hurt, your present pain, and your future journey inward."*

The Christian God, I've come to learn, is one of "with-ness." Jesus was called "Emmanuel," which means "God with us." God with you. God with me. I no longer think that God is a bearded Zeus-like figure, sitting up on his throne and planning and allowing things to take place in the world; rather, I think he's *with* us always, even in the things that happen to us that have no explanation. As Jesus says in Matthew 28:20, before his ascension, "And surely I am with you always, to the very end of the age."

He is a God who proved through his son, Jesus Christ, that he longs to enter into our worlds and our sufferings. The most accurate picture of God that we have, after all, is of a suffering savior hanging on a cross. And that is why we can gain the courage to evaluate our pain: because we serve a God who needed courage himself. Again, Timothy Keller writes so beautifully in his book *Hidden Christmas*, "If you think it takes courage to be with [Jesus], consider that it took infinitely more courage for *him* to be with *you*. Only Christianity says one of the attributes of God is courage. No other religion has a God who needed courage."

Strengthened by God, may we all find the courage, may *you* find the courage, to go on a journey inward and unpack those boxes in your attic.

PART III
TRANSFORMING THE WOUND

"The way in which a man accepts his fate and all the suffering it entails, the way in which he takes up his cross, gives him ample opportunity—even under the most difficult circumstances—to add a deeper meaning to his life. It may remain brave, dignified and unselfish. Or in the bitter fight for self-preservation he may forget his human dignity and become no more than an animal. Here lies the chance for a man either to make use of or to forgo the opportunities of attaining the moral values that a difficult situation may afford him. And this decides whether he is worthy of his sufferings or not."

Viktor Frankl, *Man's Search for Meaning*

11

Dreams and a Dream Job

The Importance of Transforming

I have been a *Star Wars* fan for as long as I can remember. But it wasn't until I began writing this book that I started to see connections between my love of *Star Wars* and my personal life. I began to understand why I was perhaps subconsciously drawn to the ways of the force in the first place.

Growing up, my all-time favorite movie was *The Empire Strikes Back*, the second installment of the Star Wars trilogy. When it released, I stood in line for hours at the old Fox Theater in Colonie, New York, bubbling with excitement and anticipation. For a kid, this "galaxy far, far away" inspired my imagination and made my mind run wild.

The film was movie perfection. It had the hero (Luke Skywalker) and the ultimate villain (Darth Vader). The movie had a similar storyline to that of the Bible's David versus Goliath story—Vader and his Empire being the big bad behemoth trying to rule the world, while Luke and the Rebels played the underdog trying to restore freedom and order to the galaxy. Okay, the geek in me is truly coming out. I'll stop now.

Most of all, it had the most famous plot twist in movie history (spoiler alert!): the moment where Luke Skywalker finds out that his enemy, the man he's trying to destroy, the most ruthless villain in the galaxy, Darth Vader, is his father.

Looking back, I think this movie resonated with me on such a deep level because of the father-son conflict that existed in the film. Luke Skywalker was forced to wrestle with his emotions when he found out who his father was.

Anger. Doubt. Confusion.

I, too, battled issues of anger, doubt, and distrust of my own father (Part I of this book). What connected with me the most was watching Luke go through the process of trying to see the good in his dad. He saw someone who was flawed but not someone to give up on. Yet in evaluating the pain (Part II), he also made certain decisions for the good of himself, the Force, and the galaxy.

I, too, saw Dad as someone who was very flawed: someone who struggled with drinking, someone who struggled with addiction, and most of all someone who struggled with being a dad. Yet so much in me wanted to try and see the good in him.

And at the same time, it was *also* imperative to make decisions for the good of myself, my future, my family, and the world. It was imperative for me to transform the pain (Part III), or my life, too, could have led to destruction.

∞

One way that I attempted to transform the pain was by channeling my energy away from the hurt my dad was causing and into the pursuit of my career, my dream job.

Suffering produces all kinds of mental and emotional energy because it stretches us, but we get to choose what we do with it. Will we allow the pain to pull us backwards into unhealthy mental and emotional cycles? Or will we move forward—through the grief, into introspection, and toward purpose? We cannot control what others might do *to* us, but we get to choose what we do *with* our lives.

While at Cayuga Community College, for example—equipped to pursue my own desires because of the geographical boundary between my dad and me—I began to pursue my radio dreams for the first time. The winter of my freshman year, I became the play-by-play commentator for the Cayuga Spartans men's basketball team and even hosted an on-campus music radio show that was broadcasted on WIN 89 FM. Looking back, it was basically the lamest radio deejay show you can imagine, playing all kinds of eighties hair bands like Foreigner and Def Leppard, but I loved it and had a blast. I called the show "The Emperor's Throne" and became known on campus as "The Emperor." Seriously.

After obtaining a two-year broadcasting degree from Cayuga, I moved back to Ravena—near my father once again—and began working at a nearby hospital. Looking back, it's interesting to me that each time I was near my father geographically, my broadcasting dreams were put on pause. It does seem to demonstrate that we need boundaries if we want to foster our dreams.

While back home, Ed and I decided to reunite and room together again. We had always been perfect roommates. We got along great. We had fun. Low drama. Low maintenance.

Ed was also one of the few people I'd opened up to because I had known him for so long. In fact, one year after taking the job at the hospital, Ed and I had a heart-to-heart conversation about our futures. Neither of us were making large amounts of money (Ed was working at a bank), but we had enough to live on. We both knew, however, that we didn't want to work those jobs for the rest of our lives. And as twenty-one-year-olds, we were both seriously thinking about our long-term career aspirations. I was dead set on radio. We made a vow to one another that we would go back to school and finish our four-year bachelor's degrees.

I ended up enrolling in New Paltz (an hour away) because it had a stellar broadcasting program, and Ed enrolled in a school in Vermont. As fun as community college had been for both of us, we were reen-rolling in school with one goal in mind: to get our degrees so that we would be better positioned to pursue what made us feel fully alive. It was a business trip. Get in. Work hard. Get out.

And two years later, both Ed and I were graduating from our respective colleges with our bachelor's degrees.

Upon graduating, I had hopes of finding an on-air radio position. So I applied to at least fifty radio stations around the United States. Unfortunately, I didn't hear back from a single one.

Determined to do anything I could to get a job in the radio business, I printed out a stack of resumes and made my way around to each radio station in the area. The first place I visited was 810 WGY in Albany, New York. I took my resume, walked in, and greeted the person at the reception desk. I handed her my resume, "I will work for free here and do anything you want. Is there any chance that you have an opening?"

Though I felt incredibly desperate saying such a thing, she must've found me endearing (or perhaps felt sorry for me) because I received a phone call from the radio station the next day, offering me an opportunity to volunteer in their marketing department.

I accepted it without hesitation and worked two other jobs to help pay the bills. While working at the radio station, I was a sponge. I learned everything about how station functioned. What intrigued me the most though was producing, running a board, and being in charge of a radio show. And a few months later, a position opened up at the station for a full-time producer.

I applied and was offered the position, which entailed a salary of $15,000 with benefits. Truthfully, I would've accepted the position for a dollar. I wasn't pursuing radio for the money. I was doing it because I loved it. I had a passion for it.

A year later, I was surfing the Internet and saw that there was an open position as a producer at ESPN (yes, *that* ESPN), the worldwide leader in sports, two hours away from Albany at their headquarters in Bristol, Connecticut. I immediately applied, thinking that I had no chance in the world of getting the job. But much to my surprise, I received a phone call from an ESPN program director, inviting me to come out to Connecticut for an on-campus interview.

My interview at ESPN turned out to be the best day of my life up to that point. I walked into the main building and was directed to meet with the program director. As we sat down and began the interview, I quickly realized that I was not going to get the job. I was not qualified. Nowhere close. The requirement was five years of radio experience; I had five months. But despite the fact that I knew I wasn't qualified for the job, I was like a kid in a candy store. I was in the ESPN building; it was beyond my wildest dreams. I was sitting with someone who had the power to make me an ESPN employee. I thought, *How cool is this?*

I was in awe.

I felt alive.

The whole experience inspired me to work even harder.

After the "disappointing" rejection of not becoming an ESPN employee, I returned to my job as a producer at WGY. I *loved* being a producer there. It was without a doubt the most fun I've ever had in broadcasting. I was twenty-three years old, and the sky was the limit. Don Weeks, a local radio legend who had been on the air for thirty-some years, became a father figure in my life, teaching me everything I needed to know about broadcasting. He became a dear friend, mentor, and teacher. He really took me under his wing. I wanted to gain all the wisdom I could from that kind, genuine, and talented sixty-year-old man. He once gave me a piece of advice that I'll take to the day I die: "Remember, Jason, everyone gets old, but you can remain immature forever." What he was saying was that, just because we grow up doesn't mean that we can't have fun. He was reminding me to never take myself too seriously in the pursuit of my dream. Don died a few years back, but his legacy lives on in my memory. He will always be dear to me.

At the time that Don was having such a huge impact on me, Dawn and I were in a serious dating relationship, and we understood that I could need to move anywhere in the country on a whim if a better radio opportunity came my way. I was willing to move. Dawn was willing to come with me. Part of me also *wanted* to move to distance myself from Dad, whose alcoholism was steadily growing worse. I wanted to convert all my frustration and pain into passion and desire; I wanted to pursue radio with all my heart. My hurt only fueled my resolve to pursue my dreams—to do something *more* with my life than he was doing with his. Radio was a healthy outlet for me. So I took all the pain I was experiencing in my personal life and turned it into passion for my career.

Then, six months after marrying Dawn, I was surfing the Internet one day and came across another open position at ESPN. At that point, I'd gained two more years of experience and felt more confident in the industry. I applied once again. And about a month later, I received a call from ESPN, inviting me out for an interview, just as they had two years earlier.

This time when I walked into the Bristol, Connecticut, studios, I knew that I was a much more legitimate candidate for the job. And, after interviewing with multiple people and receiving a series of follow-up phone calls, I was eventually offered my dream job to work for "The Worldwide Leader in Sports."

I accepted immediately. I might have received a lot of bad phone calls in my life; that was one of the best. There might have been a lot of pain in my personal life, but I was using it to fan flames of my ambition as I pursued my broadcasting dreams. Though my dad struggled to hold a steady job because of his alcoholism, I was determined to not only hold a steady job but also find my *dream job*. I wanted to channel all my negative energy and turn it into something positive.

∞

Use your pain to fuel your dreams—to live in a different way than the abuser.

Over the years, I have watched the original *Star Wars* trilogy (*A New Hope, The Empire Strikes Back, Return of the Jedi*) many times. The storytelling has always been gripping to me as I've grappled with my dad's darkness and the love that I have for him. If Joe Romano was Darth Vader, then his black mask was his alcoholism. And if I was Luke, then I was forced to contemplate what it meant that someone I loved had turned into someone who lived a villainous, harmful life.

Similarly, when the prequel trilogy (*The Phantom Menace, Attack of the Clones, Revenge of the Sith*)—which essentially told the story of Darth Vader's origins—was released in the late 1990s and early 2000s, it was again extremely relevant to my life as I moved into adulthood and began to pursue my dreams in radio.

One of the most pivotal moments in the prequel trilogy is when Anakin Skywalker, a talented Jedi warrior deemed by his master Obi-Wan Kenobi as "the chosen one," begins meddling with the dark side of the Force in an effort to save his wife Padmé (because of his frequent visions of her dying in childbirth). To summarize, his despair leads to desperation, which leads to darkness. Or as Yoda might say, his fear leads to anger, his anger leads to hate, his hate leads to suffering, and his suffering leads to the dark side.

"Our inability to surrender the difficult things we might endure in life can lead to an unhealthy grappling for control, where we lose our true selves in the process and hurt other people in our path."

Things were never the same for Anakin after he ventured over to the dark side of the Force. He eventually became Darth Vader and lived the rest of his life in constant tension between good and evil, his true self and false self, passion and regret.

Strangely, it was Anakin's desire to protect and save his wife Padmé, who he dearly loved, that led to both his destruction and the traumatic distancing of himself from his two children, Luke and Leia, who he also loved. Though his love for Padmé was admirable, his boundary-lacking life—where he sacrificed his ethical code for control—led to toxic decision-making that ended up causing inconceivable harm to the Galaxy.

It is interesting to me that our desires to protect and save the ones we love, as noble as those desires might be, can also pull us into the dark side of ourselves and reality. Our inability to surrender the difficult things we might endure in life can lead to an unhealthy grappling for control, where we lose our true selves in the process and hurt other people in our path. Each challenge that we encounter in life seems to place us at a proverbial crossroads: we can surrender or try to control situation, get better or bitter, transform the pain or project it onto others.

Will the pain pull you into darkness like it did to Anakin Skywalker, or will it reaffirm your desire for good like it did for Luke Skywalker?

In his bestselling book *Love Does*, Bob Goff writes, "It has always seemed to me that broken things, just like broken people, get used more; it's probably because God has more pieces to work with." One might argue that it was Luke's brokenness—his tragic past—that fueled his goodness and his desire to bring peace into the world and fight for what was right.

Having a father who, like Vader, seemed to lack honorable and meaningful purpose and direction in life, only fueled my desire to, like Luke, live a life that was *more* honorable, *more* meaningful, *more* purposeful, and *more* intentional. I loved my dad and cared about him, but I realized early on that I couldn't dedicate my life to rescuing and saving him, just as Luke couldn't save his dad. This would ultimately have led to my destruction. My dreams and my desires to do good in the world would have gotten lost in the cycles of alcoholism and abuse. I couldn't have maintained the sacrifice of time and energy it would have taken to try to rescue someone who wasn't ready to change. So instead, I dedicated myself to living differently.

A victim can demonstrate that his or her pain is being transformed by living *differently* than the abuser. This is how we find healing. This is how our wounds can heal others—how we can heal a broken world.

12

'ESPN Radio, This is Jason'

When Pain Isn't Transformed

It was a Monday in September 2003, and I went into work at ESPN around three o'clock in the afternoon. At the time, I was a producer for a show called "GameNight on ESPN Radio." It aired from seven in the evening until one in the morning. Little did I know when I went into work that the night would become one of the more memorable workdays in my ESPN career—and not for good reasons.

It was a big night at the office. We had lots of research and preproduction that we needed to do in preparation for our radio show. The NFL season was just starting. And my favorite football team, the Dallas Cowboys, were facing Joe Romano's favorite team, the New York Giants. It was Monday Night Football. The only game on television. The whole country watching.

A couple hours into my time at work, at around five o'clock in the evening, we got a call on the main phone line at work.

One of my co-workers took the call and said to me, "Jason, you have a phone call on line three."

I expected it to be a guest returning a call or something else work-related.

"ESPN Radio. This is Jason," I said.

"Jay, it's your dad. Don't hang up."

I was stunned to hear his voice on the other end as I wasn't sure how he'd managed to call me at work, but I proceeded to talk to him anyway.

"Dad, why are you calling me at work? Is everything okay? And how did you get this number? You shouldn't be calling here."

"I just wanted to chat about the game tonight," he casually said. "Are you excited?"

109

It sounded like he had been drinking, but even if he hadn't been, I was at work and couldn't simply chat about sports. I had a job to do.

"I can't talk right now, Dad. I have a lot of work to do to get ready for the show. It's starting in a couple hours. Let's maybe talk tomorrow."

Joe immediately became angry, thus blowing his cover; he had indeed been drinking.

"Why don't you want to talk to me, Jay? Did I do something wrong? Why are you acting like this?"

I reacted as quietly and professionally as I could manage. "Dad, right now, I'm at work. I have a job to do. I can't talk. I'm sorry."

"But Jay, please…"

"Dad, I'm sorry. I have to go."

And I hung up on him.

At this point in Dad's life, he wasn't doing well. He was definitely drinking again. And as I mentioned earlier, when he fell off the wagon, one of his favorite drinking avenues was sports. That night was a big night for him and his Giants. Start of the season. Division rivalry. Monday Night Football. And it was Cowboys' head coach and former Giants' head coach Bill Parcels's first game back in Giants Stadium since his final year as the New York Jets' coach in 1999. I knew that Dad would be drinking a lot leading up to the game and during the game. I, of course, hoped that he wouldn't—but I knew it was probably going to happen.

My mind returned to work, and I tried not to think about the phone call I had just received or Joe's drinking.

But then, over the next three hours, he called back *three* more times. Since I was the producer on call and was working on a live-show broadcast, I was the one who had to answer the work phone line—and unfortunately, we didn't have caller identification.

Every time he called, I answered, "ESPN Radio, this is Jason," and the voice I would hear on the other end came from a very drunk Joe Romano.

Needless to say, I was pissed.

It was impossible for my mind to focus.

My personal life had clashed with my professional life—something I'd hoped would never happen.

Each time I heard his voice on the other end, I'd cringe and then immediately hang up the phone. I had a radio show to produce and was getting paid to produce it. That's what I needed to focus on. But his calls triggered all kinds of things within me. All kinds of emotions. All kinds of thoughts. I was very upset.

ESPN, my dream job, my escape, was supposed to be a safe space for me to do a job I loved and not worry about my father's drinking. But on this night, there was nothing I could do about it. If someone was calling about something in the world of sports, it was my job to see what the person might be calling about. If I didn't answer the phone, my boss might think that I wasn't working. Joe had pinned me in a corner.

At one point, I excused myself for five minutes during a taped segment on the show. I went into the bathroom and threw some cold water on my face, trying to compose myself. I was furious. A nightmare was unfolding before my eyes. When Joe called, I wanted to lash out in anger and scream as loud as I could to tell him how in the wrong he was. But I couldn't do that. I had to be professional. I had a show to produce and was around other people. So back to work I went.

At halftime, the Cowboys led the Giants 20-7. Dad called again, this time quickly (and drunkenly) saying to me, "Your boys are playing really well."

"I don't care if they're up fifty to nothing or how they're playing, Dad," I said. "I specifically asked you not to call. This is getting ridiculous. Unplug your phone. Don't call me. Goodbye."

And I hung up again.

It looked like the Cowboys were going to run away with the victory, but in the fourth quarter the Giants made an impressive comeback, scoring fifteen points in a row to tie the score 29-29 with six minutes left. Another classic Cowboys meltdown.

Though it was turning out to be an incredible game and therefore a great night for our radio show, I suddenly became emotionally engaged in the game. My dad had ruined my night, drunkenly calling me time after time after time, continually disrespecting my simple requests, intruding upon my boundaries, and now I could picture him joyously celebrating his Giants' comeback, recklessly drinking straight from his stupid bottle of liquor.

Once again, sports was a battleground for us. That night, all the animosity that I had for my father was transmitted onto that silly football game.

Throughout my adult life, I sometimes rooted against the Giants when my father was drinking because I knew how upset he got when his favorite teams lost, but that night at ESPN, I was *desperate* for his Giants to lose. I wanted them to lose because I wanted him to suffer.

I felt like an evil doctor or villain. It was cruel and dastardly. I knew that witnessing his anger and disappointment if the Giants lost would bring pure joy to my soul. It was maniacal. Diabolical. But it's the sick truth. I wanted that man to be in anguish. To hurt.

At the end of the game, New York nailed a thirty-yard field goal to take a 32-29 lead with eleven seconds on the clock, their first lead since the first quarter.

Again, I felt anger welling up inside of me. I could see my dad celebrating and drinking. I knew it'd take an improbable Cowboys comeback in the final seconds for the game to turn the other way.

I accepted that the Cowboys would lose and that my dad would soon be calling to rub it in my face. I braced myself to be disappointed and hear his stupid drunken voice on the other end of the phone line.

But then the Giants made a big mistake and kicked it out of bounds on the kickoff, taking no time off the clock, and giving the Cowboys the football at their own forty-yard-line after the penalty.

On the next drive, Cowboys quarterback Quincy Carter connected with wide receiver Antonio Bryant for a 26-yard completion to put Dallas in field-goal range.

Cool under fire, kicker Billy Cundiff drained a 52-yard field goal as time expired to tie the game at 32 and send it into overtime.

When I saw the ball drift through the uprights, just inside the left pole, I let out a passionate and unexpected, "YES!" right there in the production booth. Sometimes ESPN employees would cheer during games, but it was typically frowned upon in journalistic atmospheres like that. But I honestly didn't care. I knew the field goal crushed my dad. And I loved it.

Into overtime we went, and after each team punted, the Cowboys marched down the field and set Billy Cundiff up for a 25-yard field goal, which he converted.

Game over.

My Cowboys beat *Joe Romano's* Giants 35-32.

I was ecstatic, hollering and pumping my fists, smiling from ear to ear.

Though I was always happy when the Cowboys won, that night my elation was not normal joy arising from a Dallas victory. Oh no, it was a sick, twisted sense of joy. I was in a state of anger and revenge. And I was even glad that the Giants came back and made it a game, because I knew it hurt my dad even more that they then blew it. It was a game they should've won—had they just not kicked it out of bounds at the end of regulation. His team blew a game, and that, to me, was the perfect form of suffering.

That's what you get for calling and harassing me, I thought to myself.

About an hour later, as I was getting ready to head home, the work phone rang one last time. It was close to one o'clock in the morning, and nobody was calling work at that time, so I knew exactly who was calling. It was Joe Romano. I was ready.

"ESPN Radio. This is Jason," I said cheerfully.

"Hey Jay, it's—"

But I cut him off.

"*Five* times, Dad. You called me *five* times at work tonight. This is ridiculous. This cannot happen. You have to stop this. It's one thing for your drinking to affect me, but you're affecting my work now. That can't happen. Please do not call here anymore."

I became very fatherly-like. I was in control. He wasn't in control. I talked to him like he was a little kid.

And just to get one more mean jab in, I continued, "Oh, and by the way, I'm glad your Giants blew that game. They stink, and I hope they lose the rest of their games this year."

I shouldn't have said that last line. I knew it would break him, but I honestly did not care.

Then it was his turn.

"F*** you, Jason!" he screamed. "F*** you, and f*** your stupid football team. You got some nerve. I hope you and your f***ing Cowboys both go away and die."

And then I hung up the phone before he could say another word.

That was it for me.

I couldn't believe what I had just heard.

My own father had told me that I should die.

For the first time in my life, I discovered a *hatred* for my dad. I didn't want him to be a part of my life anymore. I was ready to move on. I was done. And for a number of months, I didn't say a single word to him.

∞

I wish I could say that this ugly incident with my dad was a one-time thing, but the truth is that for the next several years, our pains continued to be transmitted onto sports. Nine years later, for example, I went on a "guys' trip" to Pittsburgh with two of my good friends, Scott and Roy, to watch a Redskins-Steelers game at Heinz Field during Robert Griffin III's rookie year. The Cowboys and Giants were playing one another after the Steelers game, so, since Scott and I were both Cowboys fans, we'd made plans to watch that game in the hotel.

Again, much like their matchup nine years before, the game went down to the wire—but this time it was Dallas who lost in heartbreaking fashion, losing 29-24 after trailing 20-0 in the first half, unable to complete the comeback.

While sitting at a restaurant after the game, my cell phone rang.

It was Joe Romano.

Scott, who had a good understanding of my situation with my dad, said to me, "Jay, don't answer it."

I ignored the call.

About five minutes later, however, my cell phone rang again. Once again, it was him.

This time I couldn't resist.

I picked up the phone.

Though this might sound like a strange thing to do—opening myself up, once again, to Joe's abuse—you must understand that when you have so much tension *with* someone and anger *towards* someone, you are always looking for a release. All I needed was an excuse to get into it with him. And if he was calling me drunk, that's all I needed to yell at him and talk down to him and treat him horribly.

"Yes, Dad," I said, picking up the phone.

"How about them Cowboys?" my dad laughed, in a drunken stupor.

"You know, Dad, congratulations on your team winning, but I can't talk to you right now."

"Why can't you talk to me? Your team blew it."

"Because every single time our teams play, you drink, and I'm tired of it. This is really becoming a problem, Dad, a big problem for you."

He went into full maniacal laughing mode.

"Wasn't it great watching your team choke their asses off?"

"Dad, I don't want to talk football with you."

"You know Eli is better than Romo, right?"

"I can't do this, Dad."

"You know what, Jason? F*** you."

And then Joe Romano hung up the phone.

That was probably the thing that upset me the most—that he was the one who hung up. I didn't like it when he had the final say, when he was the one in control, when he was the one going on the attack.

Just as my professional life at work had been invaded nearly a decade before, this time my personal life with my friends was invaded. And part of it was my fault. I was unable to let go of the pain and unable to truly forgive, and I was always looking for an opportunity to strike back at my dad and tear him down. Whereas in some ways I was able to take the negative energy from the situation with my dad and turn it into something positive, in other ways—particularly when I was blindsided by his attacks—I was unable to create space to adequately feel the pain, evaluate it, and transform it.

∞

Pain that is not transformed will always exist.

Though I had taken my past pain and used it to strengthen my resolve in the pursuit of my dreams and in the pursuit of living differently than my dad, at that point in my life, I was failing to transform the ongoing hurt Dad caused. Author Richard Rohr says, "If we do not transform our pain, we will most assuredly transmit it." And I kept transmitting my hurts onto something as silly as sporting events.

"I needed to fully feel my pain and carefully evaluate it, but instead I kept reacting to the pain or transmitting it in an unhealthy way."

The Bible says, "Love keeps no record of wrongs" (1 Corinthians 13:5), but that's not what I was doing. I loved my dad, but I was keeping a record of all the wrongs he committed.

The stories in this chapter are examples of my inability to transform the pain and how I was naturally transmitting it. At the time of both of those football games, all the hurts, disappointments, betrayals, and feelings of abandonment my father had caused were piling up inside of me—and I had no idea what to do with them. I needed to fully feel my pain and carefully evaluate it, but instead I kept reacting to the pain or transmitting it in an unhealthy way. I often tried to mask my pain, hide it, or even lash out at my dad by making "he's calling again" a game of getting even with him. Later in my life, this was often why I would still pick up the phone when he called—I had so much emotion built up within me that I wanted to lash out at him. Now, as a Christian, I can see that I was very immature in my approach to my dad for many years—and it was because of the pain that I had experienced, a pain that I didn't know how to handle. *What was I to do?*

13
The Father I Never Had

Transforming Pain Through Learning to Suffer Well

I have already mentioned how special Dawn's and my wedding day was. To have found the love of my life in Dawn—someone who accepted me as I was, my scars and all, my family and all—was something that I hadn't been sure I'd ever find. Yet there she'd been at the altar, vowing to spend the rest of her life with me.

Our wedding day was special for another reason.

It was the beginning of our journey to become parents.

We knew that having children was on the immediate horizon. Our wedding day was a celebration of my public vow to the love of my life, but it was also a celebration in anticipation of our familial journey. Dawn and I were both ready to become parents.

As you might imagine, my deep-seated longing to be a father was one that was born out of unfathomable pain from my past. I wanted to redeem the difficulties from my childhood through my own parenting. I wanted to be the father I never had. I wanted to break the chain of addiction and play my part in returning the Romano family to the loving, honorable ways of Nana and Pa.

Pursuing my career dreams was one way of transforming the wound that Joe left. My desires to raise a family were another. Though I couldn't control whether or not Joe lived a life of meaning and purpose, I *could* control how I chose to live. Though I couldn't control if Joe ever found the healing we all wanted for him, I *could* control how I raised my family—how we would be a force for good and love in the world.

So upon getting married, Dawn and I immediately began planning for a family.

However, a few months went by, and we hadn't gotten pregnant yet. Considering it takes most couples at least six months to get pregnant,

117

we weren't at all concerned.

It was also during this time that my brother Chris and his middle-school (seriously, middle school!) sweetheart, Tara, were wedded. They immediately got pregnant—on their honeymoon, actually. It was a surprise baby, but they were ecstatic when they found out that they were expecting. Chris, too, was looking for redemption.

In June of 2000, Chris's son, Samuel—my mom and dad's first grandchild—was born. I remember my father being there at the hospital—sober, too—and it was a special moment for my whole family. Though Joe had missed almost every single important aspect of my life, it was good to see that he was there for my brother.

Deep down, however, I was jealous—not because my dad was there—but because I wanted a child, too. We'd been married for eight months and had not yet conceived.

Time continued to pass.

A year went by.

No children.

In March of 2001, Chris called me and shared with me that he and Tara were pregnant again. They had their second child, Hannah, in January of 2002.

Another year went by.

No children.

In June of 2002, my little brother Damian got married. One month later, I was in Milwaukee covering the MLB All-Star game for ESPN, and I received a call from him.

"Are you sitting down, Jay?" Damian asked me.

I was in my hotel room, so I sat down in a desk chair.

"Linda is pregnant," he said, talking about his wife.

Another honeymoon baby.

Both of my brothers.

Why was it so easy for my brothers to have children but so difficult for me?

Without thinking, I said, "You gotta be kidding me."

It was definitely an inappropriate response and one that seemed to catch him off guard. And understandably so.

But it came out of a deep place of pain, and what I said was actually more directed at God than to Damian. I was keeping score in my head.

God, that's three kids for my brothers and zero for me. Why are you do-

ing this to me?

I was happy for Damian and Linda, of course, but I was angry with God—angry with life. *What were we doing wrong? What was wrong with us?*

Dawn and I decided to see a fertility specialist.

I seemed to be fine. She seemed to be fine.

Another year went by.

Nothing.

In March 2003, Damian and Linda had their first child, Olivia.

And four months later, when we celebrated Nana's eighty-third birthday at a nearby restaurant, Chris pulled me and Dawn aside after dinner and dessert and gently said to us, "Guys, this is really going to hurt, and in a sense I hate to tell you this, but we need you both to know that Tara is pregnant again."

I really appreciated Chris' sensitivity toward our situation and how he elevated our sufferings and shared the news with us privately before sharing it with anyone else.

This time I was determined to react differently.

"Man, I'm so happy for you," I tried to say genuinely. "This is so awesome. Good for both of you. We love you both."

I was beginning to think to myself, *Dawn and I aren't ever going to get pregnant, so we need to start being happy that we are going to be aunts and uncles again.*

I tried to put on a happy face, but deep down I was struggling.

∞

The sad thing about our struggle with infertility was that Dawn and I hardly talked about our anger, sadness, or grief. There was a general feeling that if you talked about it, then you were jinxing your chances of ever getting pregnant. I suppressed my frustrations, just as I had done with my dad's alcoholism for most of my life.

One thing that this struggle did do, however—which would eventually have a positive effect on my life—was take me to a place of desperation.

Years before, in 1998, my brother Chris had given his life over to Christ and was radically saved by grace and transformed. Honestly, I thought his conversion was weird at the time. He became a "Jesus freak"—and a passionate, vocal one at that.

A few years after Chris's conversion, in 2001, when Dawn and I were in the thick of our struggle with infertility, I attended church with Chris, Damian, and my mom. At Chris's house after the service, he asked me, "What did you think?"

Though I was a little spooked by the church's charismatic form of worship—which was *very* different from what I'd seen in Catholic churches—I actually really enjoyed the sermon.

"It actually wasn't that bad," I replied.

That opened up the door for him to say, "Wasn't that bad? You mean that you didn't hate it?"

We had a brief discussion and then went to the back bedroom for a much deeper conversation. There, Chris shared the gospel with me for the first time. It was a conversation that planted a seed and sent me on a journey that changed my life.

"Would you like to accept Jesus as your Lord and savior?" Chris asked me.

I didn't know much about what I was doing at the time, but Dawn's and my struggle with infertility had left me feeling lost and desperate and confused. I thought that if perhaps I could get God on my side, then maybe he'd let Dawn get pregnant. I thought that if perhaps I could check another spiritual box, then God might help me out a little more. I might've had the wrong theological intentions, but they nonetheless took me deeper into faith.

I started having spiritual conversations with Chris, watching sermons on TV, and reading Christian books. I wasn't radically transformed like my brother had been, but I casually became more interested in a more personal form of Christianity than in the traditions of Catholicism I'd known.

Two years later, God had become more than a good-luck charm. I was growing in my faith and changing as a person from the inside out. I wouldn't say that my Christian faith had become a deep part of my reality by this point in my life, but I was certainly taking it more seriously. I was attending a Bible-believing church on my own, reading daily devotions, working on my cursing (especially when my father called), and listening to Christian music.

Though I was still frustrated with our infertility, I was beginning to find a hope and joy in my faith that sustained me in my frustrations and despair.

At the start of 2003, Dawn and I decided to try a procedure called IUI (Intra-Uterine Insemination). My insurance at ESPN covered three attempts at the procedure. We thought to ourselves, *Why not give it a shot?*

In our minds, this was our last-ditch effort to get pregnant.

We tried it in January.

Nothing.

We tried it again in the middle of the year.

Nothing.

We decided that we would try it one last time in August, and if that didn't work, then we would give up on trying to have kids of our own.

It was during this time that Dawn finally began to express to me the anger that was welling up within her.

"Why does God hate me?" she asked me one evening with teary eyes.

It was a difficult conversation. I told her that God didn't hate her or us but that perhaps his plan was more mysterious than we could imagine.

By this point, I had accepted that even if Dawn and I never had children of our own, I would be okay, our marriage would be okay, and our life would still be good. This was a very difficult thing for me to accept because I wanted kids so badly. (Little did I know at the time that this level of acceptance and surrender was something that would influence me later on in my life when it came to moving toward peace and forgiveness in my relationship with my father.)

After our third attempt at IUI in August, Dawn and I had very low expectations, considering our grueling four-year struggle with infertility.

But one day in September, when Dawn was at her nine-to-five job and I was at home getting ready to go to work, I received a phone call.

"Mr. Romano, this is the nurse from New Britain Hospital. I have some news for you."

"Okay," I said hesitantly.

"I have the results of your latest test," she continued. "The results are positive. Congratulations. Your wife is pregnant."

I was shocked. I couldn't believe it. *Was this real?*

"Thank you," I said, choking back tears.

And then, after hanging up the phone, I dropped to my knees and wept uncontrollably for ten minutes straight, like I had never wept before. I kept saying, "Thank you, God," over and over and over again. Nothing else came out of my mouth.

That was the most rewarding phone call I've ever received and also the most connected to God I've ever felt. It was an answer to prayer—a prayer that I'd thought would never be answered. And then God gently said, "I told you not to lose faith."

It was the greatest feeling I've ever had—a borderline mystical and out-of-body experience where I felt like God was right there next to me. It was like feeling his love, passion, grace, and forgiveness for the first time—and all at the same time. I had come to extreme helplessness and hopelessness in the struggle; then God provided for us in such a profound way.

Behind my tears, once again, was my past and current pain in my relationship with my father. Though it wasn't the only reason I wanted to have kids, I wanted badly to be a dad because I felt like I'd never really had one. At that time of my life, Dad was continuing to hurt me, but I didn't have a parenting outlet to redeem that hurt like my brothers had.

Now, it looked like I would.

Once I gained my composure, I finally gave Dawn a call to let her know that she was pregnant. How odd is that? There I was, the husband, delivering the news to my own wife that she was pregnant.

When Dawn picked up the phone, I screamed, "We did it!"

"We did what?" she asked.

"Honey, you're pregnant," I said.

She paused and then, calm and controlled as she always is, said, "Honey, I have some work to do, but tonight we are going to celebrate."

Nine months later, our very first child, our only child, our miracle child, Sarah, was born. We've been celebrating ever since.

Dad couldn't be there for her birth because he was seeking help in a rehab facility for his depression and anxiety, a result of the alcoholism, but my other father figure—Pa, my grandfather—wrote me a note that I'll forever cherish. It said, "Your miracle child is here. Take care of your baby, Sarah Jane."

∞

Struggles and difficulties can strengthen our resolve to redeem our pain.

Though it might seem as if our struggle with infertility was unrelated to my struggle with my father, it was actually directly related.

The infertility helped me develop a construct for learning to suffer well. It took me to a deeper place. It helped me to find my faith. The frustration pushed me to the edge of myself where I was forced to finally accept that I would be okay—and not just okay, but good—if I didn't get what I wanted. Suffering pulled me into the freedom of surrender. The freedom of giving my all but in the end allowing life to unfold how it pleases. Suffering forced me to grow and to change.

The struggles and difficulties only strengthened my resolve to transform my pain *and* redeem it. If Dawn and I couldn't have children for ourselves, we could adopt. We could foster. We could pour our energy into organizations that strengthened families in our country. In this sense, as discouraging and frustrating as infertility was, it also reaffirmed my passions and the direction that I wanted to go in my life. And I had to accept that it might not look the way I'd expected it to look. The way it had looked for my brothers. The way it had looked for my friends. The way it had looked for my coworkers. I realized I could use my struggle to empower me in how I became a force of goodness in the world.

> *"Many think that redemption is found on the other side of a struggle, but what life has taught me—what faith has taught me—is that redemption is found in the struggle, in how we suffer."*

More than anything, I learned that redemption wasn't about getting results out of the pain but was more about how I reacted to the hurt. Slowly, my reactions moved from suppression to anger to sadness to acceptance—and eventually to surrender. I credit this process to my faith, which brought me a new perspective to approach the things unfolding in my life that I didn't understand.

In stories of Christ's life and suffering, we find unexpected results and conclusions. The Jewish people in Christ's time wanted a conquering king to overthrow the Roman government; instead they got a suffering savior who hung on a cross. His *reaction* to suffering, both in his own life and in the world around him is what we remember the most about his ministry. He confronted the pain of humanity through how he lived, suffered, and died. His resurrection was the divine stamp of approval that he was who he said he was.

Many think that redemption is found on the other side of a struggle, but what life has taught me—what faith has taught me—is that redemption is found *in* the struggle, in how we suffer. I love this quote in Matt Bays's book *Finding God in the Ruins*: "Ultimately all the unredeemed really want is to know that they are capable of being redeemed in some way—that even if we have been pawned off by random life circumstances (their family of origin, past mistakes, simple human nature) we still have it in us to morph into something beautiful and useful."

Redemption is attained not through results but through how we live.

And living inevitably involves suffering.

14

My Grandfather, My Hero

*Transforming Pain Through What We Give
to Those We Love*

As my dad's alcoholism worsened throughout my twenties and
thirties, there was always one man my brothers and I could count on:
George Romano. Pa. Without a doubt, the greatest human being we've
ever known.

Not only did Pa and Nana help set us on the right trajectory in our
youth, but as my brothers and I became adults, married, and started
our own families, Nana and Pa continued to be a refuge for us.

Being men, I think my brothers and I were all especially drawn to
Pa and how he lived—how he set a different example for us than Joe
Romano did, and how he was consistent, loving, stable, and generous.
He helped to fill the void that his son, Joe, left in our lives. He gave
us a model for the kind of husband and father that we each wanted to
become. As we grew older, we realized that the path we could take as a
Romano was crystal clear: we could either become like Joe or like Pa.
And the pain that Joe caused only strengthened each of our desires to
live like Pa.

On the day after Thanksgiving in 2007, I had a conversation with
Pa that I'll remember for the rest of my life. Though he couldn't be
at our Connecticut home with my family and my brothers' families
for Thanksgiving—as he was spending it visiting Nana in the nursing
home—we passed the phone around the table and each spent time
talking to him. It was a special moment—to see everyone talk one-on-
one with this man who had always held our family together.

When it was my turn, I talked to him about what we always talked
about: sports. I think he took a lot of pride in the fact that he had a
grandson employed at ESPN. We talked about the Packers (his favorite
team) and the Cowboys, who were playing one another the following

week. We also talked about the Celtics, who had acquired Ray Allen and Kevin Garnett in the offseason and who were playing that evening. Pa had passed his love for sports down to my dad, and my dad had passed it down to me. It was a normal conversation, but it was one that I really enjoyed.

That was the last time I ever spoke with Pa.

Merely one day after the Cowboys played the Packers on Thursday Night Football—one week after that last conversation with my grandfather—I received a call from my brother Damian.

"Jay," he said desperately, "Pa is missing."

"What?" I asked, shocked.

"No one has heard from him. He's not answering our calls."

Damian was flustered and wasn't making any sense.

"Well, maybe he's just not picking up his phone."

Twenty minutes later, I received another phone call from Damian.

"Pa is dead," he said.

My knee-jerk reaction was to deny it. "No, he's not," I said. "I don't believe you. I don't believe you. I don't believe you at all."

But it was true. The greatest man I ever knew: gone.

Apparently, my brother Chris had found Pa in his Ravena home, on the floor next to his bed, lifeless. His television had been tuned to ESPN. It made me wonder if he had passed away watching the company that I had worked for.

And it was almost as if God had orchestrated that Thanksgiving weekend call for each of us to talk to him one last time.

In the week leading up the funeral, in a bizarre moment, Mom, Dad, Chris, Damian, and I all found ourselves in the same vehicle, riding to the funeral home to set up arrangements for Pa. "Well, this is the happy family we all wanted, huh?" I remember saying. It was a moment of levity, but beneath the humor was also a lot of truth and therefore some pain.

I found myself thinking about a lot of things that week—and I think my brothers found themselves doing the same. *How could I live more like Pa lived? How would his legacy extend in the Romano family through my brothers and me? What if Dad died—would anyone show up at his funeral? Did Pa die with a broken heart because of his son's alcoholism?*

To Dad's credit, he was really strong that week. Though he was enlisted in a rehab facility, as his alcoholism was in a tailspin, the people at the facility allowed him to leave for the funeral. I really thought that he was going to lose it when he found out that his father had passed away. You know, back to the drinking, back to the depression. But he didn't.

Dad was a rock for all of us the entire week, the father we'd always hoped to have to lean on. It was as if he was channeling his inner Pa, something we'd always known that he had in him. And for perhaps the first time in our adult years, our own father acted like a father.

The entire experience was a surreal picture of two generations of men in our family and the dramatic differences in their lifestyles. I hoped that Dad could still turn his life around.

Pa's funeral reaffirmed what each of us hoped to become. To live the way Pa lived—the *true* Romano way. Maybe it had skipped a generation, but it was still moving to each of us that such a loving, inspiring man and such a dedicated husband and father was the patriarch of our family.

The whole town of Ravena seemed to show up at his funeral. See, he wasn't just "Pa" to us—he was "Pa" to the entire village of Ravena, to hundreds of people who his life had touched. Though Pa wasn't much of a vocally religious person, he lived a grace-filled life through his actions.

We buried him in his beloved Green Bay Packers jacket.

At Pa's wake, I was the first one to stand up and speak. As the oldest grandson, I had written a letter to Pa that I wanted to read. I told my brothers ahead of time that they might have to help me read it if I broke down. I couldn't help but think of the time that I'd stood up and spoke at Nana and Pa's fiftieth wedding anniversary and kept choking up. This time it was no different; I kept choking up. But somehow I fought through it and made it to the end. The letter, from December 3, 2007, had a few interesting lines that I would like to share with you:

Hearing about your death came as a shock to me because I couldn't imagine a single day in my life without you alive in it. You were the single greatest person I've ever known...

You were my grandfather, but you were also my friend. You

were my second father, and in many cases you were my first father... Your example of love and grace is one that I want to continue to emulate for the rest of my life... You loved your wife unconditionally for sixty years and visited her every single day when she was bound to a nursing home. You loved in a way I'm not sure I've ever seen from anyone in my entire life. You gave and gave and gave and never asked for anything back...

The Bible talks about our lives being a living example of what Jesus was all about, and Pa, that's what you were. You were a living example of someone who loved unconditionally, who gave unconditionally, and who touched many, many, many lives along the way. That is called a legacy, Pa, and you left one for all of us...

I only pray that my life, my marriage to Dawn, and my relationship with Sarah can be half as good as what your relationship to Nana and your love for Chris, Damian, Mom, Dad, and myself was...

Pa, I dedicate the rest of my life to you and your memory. I will love you forever.

∞

Suffering can strengthen our desire to give, love, and serve.

A few years ago, we all traveled to Damian's house in Raleigh, North Carolina, for Thanksgiving. After a wonderful dinner, something odd happened. All our children were playing with one another, scattered around the house. Our wives were all in another room. My mother's husband, Ron, was elsewhere. And it was just Mom, Dad, Chris, Damian, and me in the kitchen together. Just the five of us.

The last time just the five of us had shared the same space had been when we were in that car over a half-decade before on the way to the funeral home to make arrangements for Pa. And before that, it had to have been at least three decades before, when Mom and Dad were still married. Whatever the case, the moment felt like a kiss from heaven. A kiss from Pa, perhaps. A reminder to me that my brothers' lives and my life are unfolding miracles.

Today Chris and Damian are unbelievable husbands and fathers. Chris has four kids. Damian has four. Dawn and I have our daughter. Each of us has dealt with our own set of challenges—in our marriages, in our parenting, in our past wounds—but, without a doubt, I can affirm that we have carried on

> *"And for my brothers and me, our greatest weaknesses— what we endured as sons—became our greatest strengths—what we* give *as fathers."*

Pa's legacy thus far. And that might be the most meaningful thing I could ever say about my family.

In Thornton Wilder's short play *The Angel That Troubled the Waters*, there is a profound line that has been quoted in many Christian books: "Without your wound, where would your power be?" And for my brothers and me, I'm confident that the wounds our father caused led to a certain power for each of us—a determination and dedication to live and parent the right way.

As Bob Goff writes, "Things that go wrong can shape us or scar us." And for my brothers and me, our greatest weaknesses—what we endured as sons—became our greatest strengths—what we *give* as fathers.

Our wounds strengthened our direction and willpower to be even better husbands and fathers. To live and to love the way Pa lived and loved. To hope the way he hoped. To believe in our father the way Pa believed in his son.

It has been a difficult road, but I think that Pa would be proud.

I miss him every day.

15
Blessing in Brokenness
A Spiritual Take on Transforming

"Surely he took up our pain
and bore our suffering,
yet we considered him punished by God,
stricken by him, and afflicted.
But he was pierced for our transgressions,
he was crushed for our iniquities;
the punishment that brought us peace was on him,
and by his wounds we are healed."
Isaiah 53:4-5

"The Lord is close to the brokenhearted
and saves those who are crushed in spirit."
Psalm 34:18

"Whoever finds their life will lose it, and whoever loses their
life for my sake will find it."
Matthew 10:39

I have come to believe that enduring life's difficulties—and learning from them—is how we become agents of healing in the world. It is in the darkness where God's love, grace, and hope shines brightest. Where we connect with others at a deep level. Where we let one another know that we are not alone. Where God does his finest work. Where true blessing is born—if not for you, then for others.

It was a long, difficult process for me to be able to see that there was blessing that could come from my own brokenness—that there was beauty that could be born out of my deepest pains, that there was good that could come from so much bad. I learned that whenever I allowed myself to move past the unfairness and partnered with God to use my brokenness as a channel for good, I began to see the pain transform:

Into an undying pursuit of sports radio that led to my dream job (Chapter 11).

Into a beautiful Christian faith birthed from the ashes of my sorrow—something that would bring me so much hope, joy, peace, and perspective throughout my life—and a relentless desire to become the father I never had (Chapter 13).

Into an even deeper understanding of togetherness and the importance of family—an unbreakable bond between my brothers and me, our wives, and our children (Chapter 14).

The hurt and all the crazy things that continued to happen as my dad's alcoholism got worse and worse (Chapter 12) became fuel for me to fulfill my purpose. As Victor Frankl says in his book *Man's Search for Meaning*, "In some ways suffering ceases to be suffering at the moment it finds a meaning, such as the meaning of a sacrifice."

It was during my young-adult years that I finally began to ask myself: What do I want this pain to turn into? Though I still don't understand why Joe did what he did and though I still harbored a lot of bitterness toward him and had yet to forgive him in my twenties and thirties, I finally realized that my pain would be pointless if I didn't allow it to become something positive for others.

Never in my wildest dreams did I imagine the freedom and joy I'd experience in such a negative sounding word as "brokenness."

∞

God can use our pain as a means of bringing more peace into the world.

Isaiah 53:5 states, "But he was pierced for our transgressions, he was crushed for our iniquities; the punishment that brought us peace was on him, and by his wounds we are healed."

Christ's physical, psychological, and emotional wounds brought healing into the world. He was brutally crucified on a Roman cross, and by accepting this death, he showed how deeply God loved the world. He was rejected and slandered and betrayed by the very people he came to serve, and by enduring their insults, he showed how relentless God is in the pursuit of those he loves.

The life of Christ is the prime example of bringing blessing through brokenness. He had "no place to lay his head" (Luke 9:58), "made himself nothing by taking the very nature of a servant, being made in human likeness" (Philippians 2:7), and "being found in appearance as a man, he humbled himself by becoming obedient to death—even death on a cross" (Philippians 2:8).

He taught of countercultural paradoxes—how you have to lose your life to find it (Matthew 10:39), how God's power is being perfected in our weaknesses (2 Corinthians 12:9), and how it is more blessed to give than to receive (Acts 20:35). A common narrative in Jesus's teaching is an "emptying out" of oneself for the good of one another.

All these lessons were profound in Jesus's time, and they're just as relevant today as we wrestle with similar cultural and societal struggles in America. Hierarchal oppression. Religious oppression. Racism. Sexism. Public shaming and outrage.

Jesus, however, provided an alternative example of what it meant to be fully human and alive—even when he and his people were being oppressed and abused by the Romans. In fact, their sad circumstances in that society are what made Jesus's teaching and his apostles' way of life even more radical.

"If we have not evaluated our own wounds, it is difficult to guide others toward healing. When moving toward forgiveness and peace, we can only go as far with others as we have gone within ourselves."

After Christ's resurrection, his apostles' lives reflected the countercultural, profound way that he lived. It was through *weakness* and *brokenness* that the early church was born. Most of the apostles went on to suffer horrific deaths at the hands of their oppressors. But out of this, a spiritual revolution and movement was sparked. Their deaths gave validity to their radical lifestyle of selfless love that Christ taught them. Beauty flowed out of brokenness.

But allowing beauty to bloom out of the soil of brokenness is challenging because it means being in touch with our weaknesses. You cannot discover the power of your wound if you do not fully feel it or dare to evaluate it. Once you step into awareness, however, I think true internal transformation can begin to unfold.

That's the purpose of being in touch with our brokenness. Even though introspection and evaluation can be painful and challenging, it's difficult to step fully into joy until we get to the bottom of the pain. In addition, if we suppress our own pain, it is difficult to relate to others when they are feeling their deepest pains. If we have not evaluated our own wounds, it is difficult to guide others toward healing. When moving toward forgiveness and peace, we can only go as far with others as we have gone within ourselves. Our healing is not only for ourselves; it is also for the others we encounter.

Every hero of a story has something that he or she must overcome. Once a hero has dealt with his or her ghosts, he or she becomes a guide for others' heroic journeys.

Throughout my early adult years, God helped me transform my deepest pains. As crazy as it sounds, I even began to see the good that could come from my own challenging situation with my dad. But the final step of my journey—forgiveness—was yet to begin.

My dad's alcoholism and abuse might have been fueling my resolve to pursue my dreams to live a loving, Christ-centered life and to be the best husband and father I could become, but I had no idea how to truly forgive that complicated, confusing man. I had no idea how to love him. His sins were ongoing. His alcoholism was worsening. Whenever my relationship with him seemed to be on an uptick, it would then suddenly plummet. Some of the decisions he made throughout my adult years, like when he repeatedly called me during the Giants and Cowboys games at ESPN, truly made me hate him. And that wasn't even the tip of the iceberg. He often made my life miserable, and he wouldn't stop.

Transforming my pain was one thing. Truly forgiving Joe Romano when I often wished he was dead—well, that was another.

PART IV
FORGIVING THE ABUSER

"To be a Christian means to forgive the inexcusable, because God has forgiven the inexcusable in you. This is hard. It is perhaps not so hard to forgive a single great injury. But to forgive the incessant provocations of daily life—to keep on forgiving the bossy mother-in-law, the bullying husband, the nagging wife, the selfish daughter, the deceitful son—how can we do it? Only, I think, by remembering where we stand, by meaning our words when we say in our prayers each night 'forgive us our trespasses as we forgive those that trespass against us.' We are offered forgiveness on no other terms. To refuse it is to refuse God's mercy for ourselves. There is no hint of exceptions, and God means what He says."

C.S. Lewis, *The Weight of Glory*

16

From Football to Baseball

The Importance of Forgiving

Imagine getting closer to someone you love—say a parent or a spouse or a significant other—but every step you take toward the person, addiction pulls him or her two steps further away. Every time you catch a glimpse of what "could be," it is ripped away from you.

This kept happening with my father and me, and it really took its toll. Frustration, anger, and bitterness toward my dad grew within me.

In the next several chapters, I have allowed some of the raw emotion that I felt at the time to exist in these pages so the reader can perhaps feel and relate to the rising tension one feels when caught in a monotonous, seemingly unending cycle.

Being a Christian is at the center of who I am—at the center of being a husband, a father, a brother, a friend, and an employee at ESPN—but it wasn't at the center of my relationship with Joe Romano. I would pray for other things, and I believed that God could bring guidance and healing, but when it came to my dad, I honestly began to think that God just didn't care about me having a relationship with him. My prayers became empty prayers. My hope became hollow. I didn't think that my dad would ever change—nor did I think that God cared if he did. And because of that, my Christianity never permeated my sonship. I was bitter and wanted Joe to pay for his mistakes.

∽

In August of 2003, just a month prior to the infamous Giants-Cowboys Monday Night Football game when Joe kept calling me at work, he and I decided to attend a Cardinals (his team) versus Mets (my team) game at Shea Stadium. Though there were some real issues between Joe and me, I always seemed to let him back in. I wanted a relationship with him. That desire and longing was always there and never went away. Though Damian once shut Dad out for a couple of years, I couldn't bring myself to do it. I had personal boundaries with him, but I always seemed to leave the door cracked open. *I wanted a father.*

Leading up to the Cardinals-Mets game, I was nervous. I couldn't help but think about the game we'd been supposed to attend in my youth, seventeen years before, when I'd been so hurt by his drinking that I'd locked myself in the bathroom. This time, I was scared to death that he was going to break away at some point and get himself a drink, either at the game or on the way there.

I was apprehensive, fearful, and worried—but to his credit, he didn't have a sip of alcohol the entire time. I might not have been able to enjoy the game fully, but it was a fun time, and I was really proud of him. In a sense, it was like we were making up for the moment seventeen years prior.

It was a classic game, too. The Cardinals, who had an amazing team that year, beat the Mets 10-9. New York scored five runs in the bottom of the ninth but couldn't complete their comeback. Why did it seem like it was always a close game when our teams played one another?

You might think that the tension between us would have been high during an intense game like that, but the truth is that, even though I was a little bummed the Mets lost, the game was fun because my dad was sober. What I wanted more than anything throughout my life was his sobriety.

Around this time, I was beginning to feel like our relationship was on the upswing. I even sold him my car, a 1998 Ford Escort, soon thereafter. It was his first time having a car since he'd lost his license in the late nineties. Interestingly, when I sold him the car, I felt like I was in a fatherly role once more—discussing with him the responsibilities of driving and how he needed to be smarter and make wiser decisions. Nonetheless, it was an encouragement to me that Dad seemed to be getting his life back together again. He was excited for the freedom that having a car would give him and even had plans to get back into substitute teaching. I felt that he was beginning to return to reality. It felt like everything was on the up and up.

But although our relationship got better quickly, it fell apart even quicker.

∞

I never should have sold my car to Joe Romano.

After a few months of sobriety, he began drinking again.

Months later, he got another DWI—his third—after running through a four-way stop near Albany and crunching my former car into a BMW. Thankfully, no one was injured, but my dad was arrested on site. His blood alcohol level was reported at twice the legal limit. Once again, Dad was spiraling out of control.

The next day at work, I read a story about him on a local news site, and I watched a video of a newsman reporting on the accident who said, "Joe Romano was arrested…" That was one of my worst personal experiences with his alcoholism. Knowing that a story like that about my own father was on the Internet and accessible to the entire world was humiliating.

I shook my head and tried to forget about it. I emailed the link to my brothers because I knew that they would understand. In the email, I included these words: "I hope this is rock bottom for him." It was humiliating to see Dad on the news, but I had hope that it would be his wakeup call.

Not quite.

He was bailed out of jail by a local bar owner, and he quickly returned to his binge drinking.

Nothing changed.

And this frustrated my brothers and me to the core.

We had heard that there was a chance he might have to go to jail because the person he hit, the owner of the BMW, had a lot of money and was pressing charges, but I figured he would get off the hook, just like he always did. All he ever seemed to get for his reckless decision-making was a slap on the wrist. He would squeak by any legal issues and continue to live on his disability pension, which fueled his addiction.

Oddly enough, it was around this time that the Mets and Cardinals were facing off in the National League Championship Series. The Mets had notched the best record in baseball during the regular season, and although the Cardinals had barely made the playoffs, they were on a roll in the post-season. It was the Mets' first time in the NLCS since 2000, and it was the Cardinals' fifth trip in six years. I was dreading the series because I knew that Joe would be drinking during each game and calling me. I imagined the avenue of athletics would once again become a battleground for us to release our built-up tension.

That time, however, it was different.

You might think that I would have been rooting hard for the Mets throughout the series like I did for the Cowboys back in 2003—wanting my dad to be in pain, wanting him to suffer—but part of me truly felt that if the Mets won, it might totally break him, that it might be his final straw. The postseason excitement for the Cardinals combined with the depths of Dad's alcoholism made me fear that he might kill himself if the Mets won. I know that must sound crazy, but when he was drinking, he was manic. Unpredictable. Desensitized. Not to mention he had his DWI charges hanging over his head, and he was facing looming financial issues from the accident as well as the possibility of ending up back in prison. It was a fragile state for him—even more fragile than usual.

Of course, the series was as close as you can possibly imagine and went the distance—to the seventh and deciding game.

Dad called me the night before Game 7, completely wasted. And throughout Game 7, I went back and forth in my mind between wanting him to suffer through a Cardinals loss and being fearful of what would happen if the Mets actually pulled it off.

The game turned out to be a nail-biter—one for the ages. It was tied 1-1 heading into the ninth inning, and then the Cardinals' Yadier Molina hit a two-run homer in the ninth to power the Cardinals to victory.

I went to bed with a strange taste in my mouth, going back and forth in my mind between bitterness and relief, anger and confusion. Lying in bed that night, I couldn't help but wonder if it would've been *it* for Joe Romano had the Cardinals lost. Instead, he was probably hammered and celebrating the win. *Better than dead*, I thought to myself. Then again, I couldn't help but wonder if maybe it'd be better for everyone if he were dead. He made all our lives miserable.

I didn't sleep very well that night.

∞

Moving toward peace and forgiveness is a process that often returns us to the different stages of grief. It's okay if the process unfolds slowly or if it feels like you are moving backwards.

I always thought that I had forgiven my dad. Especially once I became a Christian back in the early 2000s and started learning about the love and forgiveness that was exemplified in Christ's life. But now I can see that back then I wasn't even remotely close to moving on and letting go of the past. I wanted to forgive, but at the same time I didn't want to because of the hurt.

In Timothy Keller's book *Counterfeit Gods,* he brilliantly says, "God's grace and forgiveness, while free to the recipient, are always costly for the giver. From the earliest parts of the Bible, it was understood that God could not forgive without sacrifice. No one who is seriously wronged can 'just forgive' the perpetrator....But when you forgive, that means *you* absorb the loss and the debt. You bear it yourself. All forgiveness, then, is costly."

I had definitely not arrived at a costly place of forgiveness. The process was still unfolding for me. It was sometimes frustrating to find myself in my mid-thirties, just as aggravated and distraught and angry and traumatized as I'd been as a little boy, screaming at my dad from the floor of my grandparents' bathroom. But peace and forgiveness aren't bound by formulas. The process of forgiveness can shift violently back and forth between feeling and expressing and transforming and forgiving. Sometimes it unfolds on multiple levels at the same time.

"It's easy to become aggravated when we return to an emotional or mental state that we thought we'd moved beyond...And once we feel something—whether it's an old emotion resurfacing or something entirely new—it is our job to evaluate that feeling and where it is coming from."

I was recently given the opportunity to preview the faith-based film *I Can Only Imagine,* which was directed by Jon and Andrew Erwin and is based on the life of MercyMe lead singer Bart Millard. Millard, as I mentioned earlier, also had a complicated relationship with his alcoholic and abusive father, and the movie focuses on that tumultuous relationship. In one scene, Millard's father, played by Dennis Quaid, says something along the lines of, "Do you think God could ever forgive me for what I've done?" The actor who plays Millard responds, "I believe that God can forgive you, but I can't."

That's exactly how I felt. I felt that God could forgive my dad, but me? No way. Not happening. I didn't even know how to forgive him if I wanted to. I was just as angry with him as I had always been. Though I was growing incredibly in my faith, my frustration with him felt the same as it always had.

It's easy to become aggravated when we return to an emotional or mental state that we thought we'd moved beyond. But there is no timeline for grief and forgiveness, and trauma reveals itself in different ways, directly and indirectly. And once we feel something—whether it's an old emotion resurfacing or something entirely new—it is our job to evaluate that feeling and where it is coming from. Time and time and time again. It might seem monotonous, but the truth is that the cycle leads us deeper into an awareness that will benefit us.

In this sense, the process of moving towards forgiveness is *always* unfolding—always moving toward repair. I think that's why when Peter asks Jesus in Matthew 18, "Lord, how many times shall I forgive my brother or sister who sins against me? Up to seven times?", Jesus profoundly responds, "I tell you, not seven times, but seventy-seven times." Jesus's words here were not meant to be taken literally; instead, they hint at the unending, lifelong process that forgiveness entails.

Sometimes my father directly wounded my brothers and me—through his phone calls, through his degrading comments, or through his reckless and toxic behaviors that affected our families—but other times we were indirectly wounded when we were reminded of the pain he caused us—say, through a conversation with a friend, through watching a movie, or through watching a sporting event. The pain was always there.

Forgiveness was easier said than done. As C.S. Lewis writes in *Mere Christianity*, "Everyone thinks forgiveness is a lovely idea until he has something to forgive."

17
Letters from Jail
The Crossroads of Forgiveness

There are few things more frustrating than experiencing a seemingly never-ending cycle. For decades, I felt like my relationship with Joe Romano went in phases: he would start drinking, and then I would get angry and disappointed and push away; he would go to rehab, and then our relationship would begin to heal because of the time apart and the distance between us; he would return to his apartment and stay sober for a period of time, during which we would continue healing our relationship through phone calls and occasionally hanging out; and finally he would start drinking again, say mean and hurtful things, and the wound that had started healing would be repunctured, and the cut would go deeper. And what's worse is that I felt like this cycle never reached its end; it just continued over and over and over again.

Building on last chapter's storyline, after the Cardinals defeated the Mets in the NLCS, they went on to win the World Series, which included lots of libations for my father. Not only that, but he continued drinking all the way through April, refusing to change as he awaited the ruling and details surrounding his DWI. He had a little motel room near Albany, and he would drink there every single day. As Dad had told me before, once a drop of alcohol gets into an alcoholic's bloodstream, it takes total control over that person. It was sad to watch. I continued to distance myself from him. I guess you could say that *I* was the one who hit rock bottom.

I was done. Helpless. Spent. Exhausted.

I wrote him a letter at around this time, asking him not to call me. I told him that if he wanted to talk to me, he could write to me. In the letter, I told him that he had a major problem and that I had a life to live. I had a family—a wife and a daughter—and a job that I loved.

"This is your battle," I wrote him. "I cannot be a part of it anymore. I hope you get better. And I hope that someday we can have a semblance of a relationship again. But right now I don't want to see you or hear your voice."

What would it take for Dad to finally come to the end of himself? He could've killed someone in his car accident. He could've gotten seriously injured or hurt someone else. A child could've been in the car that he hit. He had gotten lucky. He *always* got lucky. A local bar owner bailed him out of jail. He always had a next paycheck. I felt like he was the most reckless *and* the luckiest man I knew!

Months later, however, Dad found out that the criminal charges being pressed because of his DWI would result in him spending a minimum of seven months in jail. Though he was terrified—he had never spent more than a few hours in a jail cell before—my brothers and I were ecstatic. It sucked having to tell people that our dad was going to prison, but we were all hopeful that it could be his turning point.

Maybe this was when things would finally change.

Maybe this was when he would finally hit rock bottom.

What I didn't know was that Dad's struggle with alcoholism was perfectly paralleling my struggle with forgiveness.

Before Joe went to jail, I established a firm boundary: we wouldn't see one another or talk on the phone while he was there. I told him that if we communicated at all, it would be through letters. I wanted him to know that I still cared for him and believed that he could heal, but I was also at my wit's end. I also needed to detox—not from alcohol but from the heaviness of his actions.

And so, Joe Romano went to prison.

His time in jail was a great time for me personally, because I didn't have to talk to him, nor did I have to worry about him drinking. He was in prison getting clean. With ample time on his hands to think and reflect, he decided to write me letters. After I'd received four or five letters from him, I finally decided to respond.

I figured that not many people were communicating with him, and I wanted him to know that I was thinking of him and praying for him. I don't remember what I said, but in late May of 2007, I received a letter back from him. I have kept it for all these years because it's one of the most beautiful things I ever received from him.

In the letter, he was introspective and humble, apologetic and hopeful. At points, he was submissive, almost childlike in his approach. He practically begged me to do certain things. He understood how helpless of a position he was in because of the boundaries that I had established. He also talked a great deal about faith and God's will, something he had never done before. And of course, there was plenty of sports talk in there; what would communicating with my dad be *without* some sports talk? He wrote:

Dear Jay,

Hope you and Sarah and Dawn are well...

Well I guess the Celtics are still "snake-bitten." How in the hell can they end up with the fifth pick? I hope Danny-boy gets smart real quick. We need someone to aid Pierce/Jefferson. We'll see. By the way, I know you are loyal and won't switch teams, right?

Kiss Sarah for me on her birthday, ok? I really would like to talk to her on her birthday; can I call collect just this one time? [He knew I had a boundary here.]

I'm really glad you and I are communicating. As time goes on, in God's light, our relationship will get better and better. I really think the Mets will play either the Angels or Red Sox in October. Just think, after you recover from an opening-season loss to the N.Y. Giants, YOU'LL STILL HAVE THE N.Y. METS for the post-season!

Mike, who is the counselor here, is going to write me a letter of recommendation for the judge and the district attorney. Hopefully, and maybe, I will be able to finish my jail time in a rehab for a few months. This would be a blessing since I would benefit greatly with a long-term rehab. It would greatly aid my sobriety and my attitude. I pray only for God's will, not the rehab, un-

less the rehab is God's will. I ask you to pray for me, for God's will, as well.

I love you very much, and if I could take back everything I ever said that was hurtful I would. No one, especially you, deserves foul treatment. Thank you for being my oldest son and for being thoughtful. I continue to walk in God's light, and am obedient to His Word and will.

Write, Son.

Love, Dad

Because of his good behavior, his sentence was reduced, and in August of 2007, he was released from prison.

And that was when Dad walked right out the doors of the prison and into the doors of a nearby tavern.

∞

To forgive, we must first admit our powerlessness.

For so many decades, I had seen my father as the one who needed to change and heal in order for my life to be more peaceful. I thought, *If Dad could just conquer his alcoholism, then my brothers' and my deep wounds could heal.* This, however, put all the pressure on him—someone my brothers and I had little control over. It was very conditional.

By the time Dad reached his fifties and sixties and still couldn't kick the bottle, I was forced to ask some difficult questions: *What if Dad never conquers his alcoholism? What if the cycle repeats itself until the day he dies? Will I put up a barrier between him and my family? Will I still love him?*

After all, Dad had gone to prison for half a year, and in his letters, I'd seen him in the humblest, most hopeful state I'd ever seen him in, and *still* the first thing he did upon getting released from prison was go to the bar. Maybe his illness was unconquerable.

Truth is, my father's struggle with the bottle and my struggle with my father were more similar that I thought. Although his battle was an addiction and mine was not, we were both challenged to find hope and strength in our interior lives. We both faced something daunting that often felt impossible to overcome. For him, it was overcoming his alcoholism. For me, it was granting him forgiveness.

I realized that I, too, had hit rock bottom in my relationship with my father. In my struggle to move toward peace. In my struggle to move toward forgiveness.

And the gateway to change, for both of us, was to admit our powerlessness.

As you move toward peace with and forgiveness toward those who have hurt or betrayed you, consider

"Truth is, my father's struggle with the bottle and my struggle with my father were more similar that I thought. Although his battle was an addiction and mine was not, we were both challenged to find hope and strength in our interior lives."

these twelve steps of AA (I have replaced any references to alcohol with references to forgiveness). These were the twelve steps that I needed to apply to my own life for me to forgive my dad.

1. *I admit that I am powerless to forgive my loved ones who have hurt me or betrayed me; my life has become unmanageable.*

2. *I believe that a Power greater than myself can restore me to sanity.*

3. *I am deciding to turn my will and my life over to the care of God.*

4. *I am making a searching and fearless moral inventory of myself.*

5. *I admit to God, to myself, and to others the exact nature of my wrongs—my inability to see the perpetrator how God sees the perpetrator.*

6. *I am ready for God to remove all my defects of character—the bitterness and hatred that fester within.*

7. *I humbly ask God to remove my shortcomings—my failures*

to forgive and love unconditionally.

8. *I am making a list of all persons I have harmed, and I am willing to make amends with them all—all the people I projected my hurts upon or took my anger out on out of bitterness.*

9. *I am making direct amends with such people wherever possible, except when to do so would injure them or others.*

10. *I am continuing to take a personal inventory, and when I am wrong, I will promptly admit it—continually feeling, evaluating, transforming, and forgiving.*

11. *I seek, through prayer and meditation, to improve my conscious contact with God as I understand him, praying only for knowledge of his will for me and the power to carry that out.*

12. *In having a spiritual awakening as the result of these steps, I will carry this message to others who struggle to forgive and will practice these principles in all my affairs.*

I remembered when Dawn and I had struggled with having children, and I'd been forced to ask some aching questions in my powerlessness: *What if we're never able to have a child of our own—will I still ultimately be okay? Will I still live a meaningful life?*

In my situation with my dad, powerlessness again brought difficult questions to the forefront and moved me toward surrender. Powerless, once again, brought me to a crossroads.

In his book *Reason for God*, Timothy Keller expands on this "crossroads of forgiveness":

> *Forgiveness means refusing to make them pay for what they did. However, to refrain from lashing out at someone when you want to do so with all your being is agony….Many people would say it feels like a kind of death.*

> *Yes, but it is a death that leads to resurrection instead of the lifelong living death of bitterness and cynicism….Forgiveness*

must be granted before it can be felt, but it does come eventually. It leads to a new peace, a resurrection. It is the only way to stop the spread of the evil.

The road to forgiveness lay ahead of me. I had no idea how to forgive the debts that Joe Romano owed—how I could possibly let go of the bitterness—but I knew that I had to try. I knew it would be difficult and agonizing. But I also knew it was necessary.

18
Doc and Darryl
Finding Empathy for the Oppressor

As a kid, baseball was my favorite sport to play. As I mentioned in Chapter 2, the New York Mets became the team that I followed and cheered for, and their two best players at the time were Dwight Gooden and Darryl Strawberry. They played in the Mets' heyday during the mid-to-late 1980s and were two of the biggest up-and-coming talents in Major League Baseball at the time.

Strawberry was named National League Rookie of the Year in 1983, and Gooden received the same award the following year. In 1985, Gooden was the National League Cy Young Award winner, and the two of them guided the Mets to a World Series title in 1986, the organization's first since 1969.

Both of their careers, however, were eventually derailed by drug and alcohol addiction. Many baseball experts would agree that their legacies, especially Gooden's, fell far short of what they could have been.

Isn't it ironic that the people I looked up to as a kid struggled with the exact same thing as my dad? Addiction.

∞

While working at ESPN, I had the opportunity to meet many different people, including a number of famous athletes. I was always able to be professional and put my fandom aside to do my job.

But then Darryl Strawberry came to ESPN.

That was a *different* day for me.

It was the spring of 2009 and, in conjunction with the release of his book *STRAW: Finding My Way*, Darryl Strawberry was scheduled to spend a day doing the "ESPN Car Wash." The car wash had nothing to do with cars or water, by the way; it was simply what we called it when a guest visited ESPN and made an appearance on all the network's major radio and television shows. As a talent coordinator and producer at the time, I was sometimes in charge of guiding the guest from show to show throughout the day. And when Darryl Strawberry, my childhood hero, agreed to come to ESPN, I made sure that I was the one to take him around. Although some of the athletes and former athletes who visited ESPN were arrogant—aware of their popularity and stardom—Darryl was one of the kindest people ever. For example, he was stopped by a number of people inside the offices—people asking for autographs and pictures—and he graciously spent time with each person. It was a lot, and I asked him how he had the patience for all the interruptions. "Jason," he told me, "this might be the only time these people ever meet me; we might never see each other again." He legitimately understood the value of each moment.

When it was just the two of us, I found him to be humble, genuine, and inquisitive from the moment we first began talking. Much to my surprise, he immediately asked me about my family and my personal life. Knowing of his struggle with addiction and his newfound Christian faith (which he credits to helping him get his life back on track), I opened up to him about Dad's lifelong struggle with alcohol—and that became the subject of our discussion the entire day. He asked me question after question and continually brought the subject of my dad up in between shows.

Darryl had overcome his addiction and was doing amazing work for the Lord in ministry, and I could tell that his post-career platform wasn't a gimmick. It was real. There he was, sharing his broken story in order to meet me in my own brokenness. He had overcome his demons and was now giving hope to others because of what he'd gone through.

"What was it for you that helped you to overcome addiction?" I asked him at one point. Behind my question, of course, was a lot of hurt. I just couldn't understand why my dad couldn't conquer his addiction.

"Jason," he told me, "it was a lot of prayer, brokenness, going through the depths of despair, and having loved ones come alongside me. And it was God—giving my life to Christ."

"Having loved ones come alongside me."

His quote echoed through my mind.

Had I ever dared to truly come alongside my dad?

I will never forget that day, as long as I live. Not only was that the best day I ever spent at ESPN; it was one of the more personal and poignant conversations I've ever had about my dad.

For the next few years, Darryl intentionally checked up on me, either through text messages or phone calls, to ask about my dad.

∞

A couple years later, I once again came face-to-face with a sports hero from my childhood.

In August 2011, Dwight "Doc" Gooden came to Bristol for the "ESPN Car Wash," just as Darryl Strawberry had done years before. I once again let the other talent producers know that I'd love to be the one to direct Doc around ESPN.

And once again I got an entire day to spend with one of my childhood heroes.

When I met Doc, he was very reserved, quiet, and introverted. Throughout the day at ESPN, however, we got to know each other on a personal level. He honestly shared with me about his journey through addiction. Since he opened up to me, I decided to open up to him about my dad and his struggle with alcoholism. Before leaving that day, Doc said to me, "I appreciate you telling me about your dad, Jason. I'll pray for him." That was a wonderful day at ESPN. Dwight is a great guy.

A year and a half later, I found out that Doc was returning to ESPN to promote his book, *Doc: A Memoir*. Though I had left my talent-booking role and was working as a social media producer, I made sure to connect with him when he got to campus. We met up for lunch, and before saying anything else, Doc asked me, "How's your dad?"

It blew me away that he had remembered our conversation from the last time we had been together and that he cared enough to ask me about one of my toughest struggles.

Dad wasn't doing well at the time, and he and I were going through another phase of not talking to each other, probably because of another vulgar phone call or something.

"He's not doing well, Dwight," I grimaced.

Doc empathized with me then said, "Do me a favor. Give me your dad's number. I'd like to give him a call."

I was shocked.

My response was, "Really?"

He looked at me and matter-of-factly said, "Yeah, give me his number."

So I gave Dwight my dad's number and then called my dad and said, "Dwight Gooden is going to call you," to which Dad responded, "What in the world are you talking about?"

I explained to Dad that I had just spent time with Doc and had shared about our family struggles with him. The ironic thing about all this is that it happened at a time when I wasn't speaking to my dad, but once again, sports forced an interaction—this time in a positive sense.

A couple weeks later, Dwight Gooden—whose baseball career had been wrecked by his addiction—gave Joe Romano—whose family had been wrecked by his addiction—a phone call that lasted about half an hour.

I will go into more detail later, but during that two-week gap between when I called my dad and Doc called my dad, another trauma had transpired. Doc happened to call my dad at one of the lowest points of his life.

∞

To move toward forgiveness, try to see things through the eyes of the oppressor, as difficult and painful as that might be to do.

Spending time with Darryl and Doc helped me to see a different side of addiction. Not only did it encourage me to see that it was possible to overcome addiction; it also seemed to humanize the disease for me. I'd often thought of my dad as a bum or a loser or a drunk. But then I saw that two wildly successful baseball players—my childhood heroes—had *also* been plagued by addiction and had lost it all. They'd lost their families, their friends, their reputations, and lots of money, and both of them had gone to jail for periods of time.

No one was exempt from the darkness and its attempts to enslave. Not Joe Romano, a former social studies teacher from Ravena, New York. Not Darryl Strawberry, a four-time World Series champion. Not

Dwight Gooden, a three-time World Series champion. And not me, Jason Romano.

One of the biggest steps in moving toward forgiveness is daring to see through the eyes of the abuser. This can be an extremely painful step, and it cannot be forced. It takes time and patience.

I should also note that I recognized my father's abuse was merely verbal and stemmed from his addiction. I cannot begin to fathom how difficult and horrible it would be for victims of physical or sexual abuse to begin to see things through the eyes of the abuser.

In the 2017 movie *The Shack*, based on Paul Young's bestselling novel, the protagonist, Mack, encounters the members of the Holy Trinity and grieves the abduction and death of his daughter. In one scene, Mack is guided into a Cave of Wisdom, where he encounters a woman named Sophia, Wisdom personified. Sophia tells him, "Today, you are the judge. Why are you surprised? You've spent your whole life judging everyone and everything, their actions and motivations, like you could really know them."

When she says this, Sophia is not being insensitive to Mack's situation but rather is using logic to break through Mack's negative perception of people, the world,

> "Trying to see the world through the eyes of an oppressor or abuser is messy and can be agonizing, especially when it comes to trauma...It isn't for every situation. But depending on where you are at in the grieving process, it can help you to develop empathy that you never thought you had."

and spirituality. She then continues, "What about the man who preys on innocent little girls? Is that man guilty? What about his father who twisted him? Doesn't the legacy of brokenness go the whole way back to Adam?"

She's not excusing people's sins but rather is tracing them back to the people or things that may not have been their faults. In Mack's situation, for example, he learns that his daughter's abductor had had an abusive father who had done horrific things to him his entire life. This obviously doesn't excuse the abduction and murder, but it allows Mack to see that the abductor had no control of who his father was and what his father did to him. It levels the playing field, in a sense. Sadly, the abductor only continued the cycle of abuse in his family and did not redeem it.

Similarly, my brother Chris says that one of the turning points for him in his process of forgiving my dad was a "leveling of the playing field"; the realization that he was just as much of a sinner as my dad. He was just as much in need of grace as my dad. In being aware of his own sin and shortcomings—his desperate need for God's forgiveness and grace in his own life—he was freed (and more willing) to show my dad grace, although Dad did not deserve it. The Cross, in essence, helped Chris to realize that he was neither better nor worse than my dad; they were on a level playing field. Both fallen. Both sinners. And most importantly, both loved.

Trying to see the world through the eyes of an oppressor or abuser is messy and can be agonizing, especially when it comes to trauma. It isn't for everyone. It isn't for every situation. But depending on where you are at in the grieving process, it can help you to develop empathy that you never thought you had. It can help you to move toward forgiveness.

My encounters with Darryl and Doc helped me to level the playing field. Thanks to them, I began to see that my dad wasn't defined by his addiction, just as they weren't defined by theirs.

Maybe my dad, too, could become my hero.

But first I had to be open to a strange, profound idea.

19
The Lowest Low
Letting Go of Bitterness

In *Star Wars: Return of the Jedi*, there is a scene where Luke Skywalker mysteriously surrenders himself to Darth Vader, his father. Following the surrender, Vader and Luke walk side-by-side through a hallway on the Death Star and Vader says, "So you've accepted the truth?"

"I've accepted the truth that you were once Anakin Skywalker, my father," Luke responds.

"That name no longer has any meaning to me," Vader counters.

"It is the name of your true self; you've only forgotten," says Luke. "I know there is good in you."

No matter how dark things got in my relationship with my dad, I couldn't ever abandon the notion that there was still good in him.

What was Joe Romano's true self?

What was his real name?

What was beneath the mask he wore?

∞

In the half-decade that followed my dad's prison sentence, his alcoholism got worse, and I watched him suffer severely from depression—an illness that had only compounded over the years.

Unfortunately, just like I never understood my dad's alcoholism (nor dared to try to understand it), I also never understood his depression. Sometimes he'd call me and tell me that he was depressed, to which I might respond, "I don't care that you're depressed. Quit drinking." In my mind, if he could just kick the bottle, then his depression would get better.

I thought that there was a rigid, clear way to healing. It was wrong of me to have been so dogmatic and simplistic, but I guess I was just burnt out and exhausted by this seemingly never-ending struggle.

Damian and I had both established some pretty firm boundaries with Dad after he was released from prison, and geography only helped matters. Damian had moved to Raleigh, North Carolina. And my family was still living in Connecticut.

Chris and his family, on the other hand, seemed to lay out the red carpet for Dad. Chris, a pastor who is truly gifted at working with people who are suffering and going through brokenness, was further along in his journey of forgiveness than I was and had decided to pursue my father and forgive him at all costs. One of the many things I admire about my brother is his dedication to healing and redemption. Deeply ingrained in him is the outlook that he is living a blessing-filled life that he doesn't deserve. He had experienced God's unfathomable grace and love in his own brokenness, and he wanted Dad to experience that as well, through his own son.

But even Chris had his difficult moments with Dad. I specifically remember Chris telling me a story about Dad showing up drunk at his house one evening: Dad barged into the house, calling Chris every four-letter curse word in the book. Chris's whole family was there. His wife. His four kids. Obviously, Dad had crossed a massive boundary.

Considering our dad didn't have a license, nor was there a bus that went by my brother's house, it was shocking for all of them to see Joe Romano, this inebriated man, standing in their living room. Chris, completely in control of his emotions, calmly escorted Dad outside and asked him to get in his car. Dad got into the car and set his half-empty Jack Daniels bottle at his feet in the passenger seat. Chris then drove Dad back to his apartment in Albany, as Dad lambasted Chris and continued to verbally abuse him.

When they arrived at Dad's apartment, my brother snapped.

"Get out of my car," Chris yelled.

Dad grabbed his bottle and stumbled into the street.

In a moment of rage, Chris then got out of the car as well, ripped the bottle from Dad's hands, and bashed it as hard as he could on the pavement.

The bottle shattered at Joe Romano's feet.

∞

Dad began to handle his alcoholism better for a while after that instance with Chris. Maybe he could tell that we were well beyond our breaking points. When I talked to Dad during that time, however, even though he wasn't drunk, he was incredibly sad. The longer he was sober, the more time he had to think. And the more he thought about his life, the more depressed he got. The lost decades came to light. In this sense, I understood why drinking was an outlet for him. It helped him to avoid reality and numb the pain.

I think that his depression stemmed from his shame, and his shame came from the fact that he spent much of his life wrestling with alcohol and feeling like a failure. His alcoholism had cost him everything important in his life: His wife. His second wife. His job. His driver's license. His extended family. At different times, his own sons. He had very few people in his life who cared for him. Hardly any friends. Both of his parents—Pa, who passed away in 2007, and Nana, who passed away in 2010—most likely died with broken hearts because of their own son.

In 2013, his depression reached a new low. It was around this time that Dwight Gooden called him and gave him some encouragement, from alcoholic to alcoholic. Dad later told me that Dwight's call gave him a boost at a desperate time in his life.

Days later, however, Dad lost his battle with depression and tried to take his own life by overdosing on pills. The next day, I received a phone call—one of those calls that blindsides you with reality and makes your heart drop into the pit of your stomach.

"Is this Jason Romano?" asked the woman on the line.

I said that it was, and she explained that she was a nurse at St. Peter's Hospital.

"Jason," she said, "your father is in the hospital because of an attempted suicide."

The moment I heard that, I said, "C'mon, really?"—which was another way of saying, "I don't believe you."

"This is very real; he's here," she said. "I wanted to let you know that he is stable and going to live. We have him here if you'd like to come visit him."

"No, I'm okay," I responded, "but thank you for the update."

Apparently Joe had taken a bunch of pills and, realizing what he had done, had quickly dialed 911 in a moment of panic. An ambulance had arrived at his house at around two o'clock in the morning. He'd been rushed to the emergency room. His life had been saved, and we were told he would live.

I shouldn't have been surprised by the nurse's call, but I was. In the previous six months, Dad had told me a number of times that he was at the end of his ropes and that he didn't want to live anymore. He might have been sober during this time, but he always sounded terrible—trapped in the depths of despair. Still, I never thought that he would try to take his life because, honestly, I didn't think he had the guts to do it. Much like the time he called me in college and told me that he was going to do it, I figured it was an attempt of his to get attention by convincing others to feel bad for him. (My reactions were based on my overly simplistic view of his addiction.)

It took a while for me to grasp Dad's suicide attempt. I went to a Bible study that evening and told the seven people in our small group what had happened. Their reaction was worse than mine.

"I'm so, so sorry. You must be struggling," one of my friends said to me.

"I'm okay," I shrugged.

It hadn't hit me yet, the seriousness of it. This was just another dent in my armor that already had a million dents from Joe Romano's attacks.

As I contemplated the nurse's phone call, however, I was forced to ask myself some difficult questions. *How do I really feel about this man, Joe Romano, my father?*

I began to, for the first time, seriously consider if I wanted him to live.

Imagine that. I was his son and was legitimately posing the question to myself: did I want my own father to live?

The reality was that if he went on to live a long, full life, there was a good chance that his cycle of alcoholism and despair would go on and on—a good chance that I would continue receiving dramatic phone calls like the one I'd received that morning. Did I want that? Did I want him to live?

This is a weird thing to write, but it's truly how I felt.

What's even weirder is that I didn't know the answers to my questions.

∝

Once Dad stabilized in the hospital, he kept asking the doctors and nurses if there was anything they could do on their end to finish what he had originally set out to do: end his life.

I eventually gave Joe a phone call.

"Dad, are you okay?" I asked.

"I'm not," he said. "I have no interest in trying to survive. No worth. No life."

He sounded horrible, the worst I had ever heard him. Quiet. Broken. Apathetic. Worthless. Joyless. In some senses, emotionless.

For the first time in my life, I was empathetic with my father. Usually whenever something dramatic happened to him, I felt that he deserved it. But for the first time, I truly felt sorry for him. My heart broke for him. I began to see the world through his eyes. I began to grapple with his shame and despair. I began to consider what it might be like to be Joe Romano—to have such a joyful and gentle demeanor but to be constantly hijacked by anger and rage through alcoholism; to have such a big, loving heart but to be perceived by those he loved as immature, mean, and selfish because of his disease. What would it be like to feel so misunderstood? To be so defined by one's failures in life? To be known as an alcoholic—not a father or a son or a teacher or even by your own name? I had always called him Joe throughout my life, as if to distance myself from him. But that wasn't his name. He was my father. His name was "Dad."

On the phone with Dad that day, I suddenly found myself at a loss for words. For so many years, I'd ignorantly thought I knew the answer to Dad's depression and anxiety: to quit drinking. But suddenly I was overcome with sympathy for him. I met him on his level—for the first time ever.

"Dad," I said, "I'm so, so sorry. I hope you get better."

∝

The doctors eventually moved my dad to the hospital's psychiatric ward so they could figure out how to medically treat him.

He was in horrible shape. He sounded like a completely empty, pitiful soul who didn't have any life left to live.

Throughout all of this, I continued to be seized by empathy. I wondered what was happening to me. After all the problems he had caused for our family, how did I suddenly feel bad for him? I'm not sure if it was the Holy Spirit or what, but I was beginning to walk in Dad's shoes.

One thought kept coming to my mind: *I need him to know that I forgive him—for everything.* I wanted Dad to know that my posture toward him from then on would be one of unconditional love, even if he struggled with alcoholism for the rest of his life.

I had always thought that I'd forgiven my dad, but during those days, I realized that I clearly had not. I had forgiven him in the sense that I was willing to talk to him and that I still wanted a relationship with him, but my forgiveness was conditional. His alcoholism always hung over his head, and in a sense I kept it there, subtly letting him know that if he wanted a normal relationship with me, then he needed to conquer his addiction: he needed to stop drinking.

I knew what I needed to do: I had to call him and forgive him.

I was afraid to make the call—it was a declaration of surrender to God, and I knew how pivotal it was. It was also scary because I knew that from that moment on, I would be forgiving the debt my dad owed—all the hurt he had caused and would perhaps go on to cause.

Forgiving involves an immense deal of courage.

But to gain my courage, I first had to swallow my pride.

And one day while he was in the psych ward, I decided to give him a call. When he answered the phone, I heard his broken voice.

Once again, I was overcome with empathy. Usually he was genuinely excited to get a call when he was sober—*especially* one from one of his boys. But that day when I called, his answer was far from, "Hey! How about those Celtics, Jay?!" Instead his voice was very low and monotone. It was sad.

"Dad, I just want you to know that I truly do forgive you," I told him. "I'm very sorry you are going through this. But I want you to know that you don't need to worry about anything that has happened in the past. Those days are gone. It doesn't matter anymore. I forgive you."

I was done with conditions. I don't think Dad received what I said that day in its entirety because he was so broken. He said something to the effect of, "That's fine, but I just don't want to live."

Despite his state of despair, something remarkable had begun taking place beneath the surface. I was stepping into freedom. Finally, after all those years, I was beginning to let go of my bitterness. I was letting go of the conditions that I'd had for our relationship.

∞

Forgiveness sets a prisoner free, and that prisoner is you.

In the film *Hoosiers*, which I referenced earlier, there is a powerful scene between Shooter, the alcoholic, and his son, Everett, in a hospital room. It is a scene that has always moved me. Shooter is in the hospital because he got blackout drunk and passed out in the middle of the woods in the thick of winter. While the team makes its momentous run to the state championship game, Shooter's in a hospital bed.

One day, Everett decides to visit his father in the hospital.

"You doing good?" Everett eventually asks him, timidly.

"Well," Shooter hesitates, "I feel real empty inside, and, uh, I have some bad visions. Son, the other night—"

But before Shooter can even begin to apologize, Everett cuts him off: "It don't matter, Dad. You're gonna get better."

Everett then looks down at the floor, looks up, and eventually says, "In a couple months when you get out of here, we are gonna get a house, both of us." He pauses. "I love you, Dad."

"Bitterness keeps us trapped in bondage; it blocks us from loving others. Keeping track of another person's wrongs gives us false power and fake control over our relationships."

Every time I watch that scene, I am crushed. It always reminds me of my own decision to forgive my dad when he, too, was in the hospital and at his lowest low—when I finally decided to come alongside him and enter into his struggle.

Before I go on, I have a caveat: It's important to remember that forgiveness does not mean forsaking boundaries. We can move toward peace and forgiveness while still maintaining healthy boundaries, especially in abusive situations. What I'm talking about in this chapter is letting go of bitterness—the poison that eats at our souls—through forgiveness.

Just as boundaries help us take intentional steps toward mental and emotional health, so does forgiveness. Bitterness keeps us trapped in bondage; it blocks us from loving others. Keeping track of another person's wrongs gives us false power and fake control over our relationships. It brings out the selfishness in our own souls. As Colossians 3:13 says, "Bear with each other and forgive one another if any of you has a grievance against someone. Forgive as the Lord forgave you."

It's an exhausting thing to keep score, to hold conditions over someone's head. That's because, when we always make the rules, we have to scramble to make sure those rules are upheld. We play a god-like role. Do you know how tiring it is to play the role of God when you are a mere human being? Humans make terrible gods. In *Beyond Ordinary*, Justin and Trisha Davis write, "Bitterness is like picking up a stone to throw and holding on to it so you'll have ammunition the next time you're wounded."

For my own health, I decided to take myself off the throne. To surrender the situation to God. To let go of my bitterness. I felt convicted that my dad needed to know that his son loved him *no matter what*. He needed to know that his son cared about him and wanted him to stay sober and overcome his terrible disease.

Most of all, my father, my dad, Joe Romano, needed to be forgiven.

20

Healing for the Victim and the Abuser

A Spiritual Take on Forgiveness

"Get rid of all bitterness, rage and anger, brawling and slan-
der, along with every form of malice. Be kind and compas-
sionate to one another, forgiving each other, just as in Christ
God forgave you."
Ephesians 4:31-32

"This, then, is how you should pray:
'Our Father in heaven,
hallowed be your name,
your kingdom come,
your will be done,
on earth as it is in heaven.
Give us today our daily bread.
And forgive us our debts,
as we also have forgiven our debtors.
And lead us not into temptation,
but deliver us from the evil one.'"
Matthew 6:9-13

In March of 2017, I attended a men's conference called Iron Sharp-
ens Iron, where I ran into Darryl Strawberry. It was my first time seeing
him in a number of years. It was no surprise that the first thing he asked
me was, "Jay, how's your dad?"

As simple of a question as it was, it suddenly took me on a mental
journey. Here was this man, Darryl Strawberry—my child baseball hero
who inspired me as an adult to approach addiction differently—asking
me a question that used to require a complicated answer. As you've read

in this book, there were always so many dark clouds hanging over my relationship with my dad: my anger, his anger, my inability to forgive, and his inability to kick the bottle. The skies were always dark. A storm was always building.

Not this time, however.

For the first time, I could say, "He's doing really well. He's four years sober."

That was a special moment.

∞

My father's journey toward sobriety might be one of the weirder stories I've heard about overcoming addiction. Following Dad's suicide attempt and his time in the hospital and the psych ward, doctors and nurses got him on a new depression medication: Zoloft. ·

Since then, he has taken a Zoloft every morning and has never looked back. When this book was published, he hadn't had a sip of alcohol in over four years—his longest span of sobriety by far. I think the freedom he experienced from his depression through his medication only strengthened his willpower and his spirit. This might seem anticlimactic, but it just goes to show how complicated addiction can be. I couldn't be prouder of him.

What's really interesting to me is how my dad's sobriety from alcohol and mine from bitterness seemed to intersect. I'm not sure if they're truly connected, but I think our parallel journey demonstrates how we can set others free by surrendering our deepest personal struggles. I came to the end of myself, and my willingness to forgive without conditions not only set me free; it also might have set my father free. And my father's willingness to fight his struggle—to dare to live and fight and love again—is not only setting him free from addiction; it's also helping to set free those who love him.

∞

Forgiveness moves us closer to seeing through the eyes of the divine.

When we start to approach abusers' or perpetrators' sins and strug-

168

gles through their lens—with a compassion and grace toward their situation, even if we don't understand it—we begin to see those who have hurt or betrayed us through the eyes of God. When we are caught in the grip of bitterness, I think we can find the gateway to freedom in Christ's view of those who wrongfully persecuted and abused him.

Jesus, the Son of God—who was fully human and fully divine and fully capable of anything—never lashed out against the Roman guards who mocked him, tortured him, and crucified him. In fact, he went so far as to pray, "Father, forgive them, for they do not know what they are doing" (Luke 23:34).

He knew who he was and who they were because he knew who God was.

Isn't it interesting that Jesus—God in flesh, the suffering savior—never placed himself on the metaphorical throne, even though he was the king and savior of the world? Whenever I place myself on the throne, it inevitably causes anxiety. Now, that doesn't mean I need to lower myself to a place of worthlessness, where I willingly take the abuse of an oppressor and never create boundaries. But it does mean I need to awaken to the same self-worth that Jesus had for himself and see that same worth in others. As Paul writes in Philippians 2:5-6, "In your relationships with one another, have the same mindset as Christ Jesus: Who, being in very nature God, did not consider equality with God something to be used to his own advantage."

In the Christian tradition, we encounter a God who became man through the person of Jesus Christ, who helps us live a life to the full. God loved us so much that he met us right where we were, in our fallen state and broken world, through the person of Christ. Jesus's life and ministry were defined by love and suffering.

God hit the reset button through Jesus because humanity had misconstrued our perception of the divine, religion, life, ourselves, and one another. The books of Romans and 1 Corinthians talk about Jesus being the second Adam—how Christ restored our view of God (as one of unconditional love and grace), our view of ourselves (as people who are deeply loved by God regardless of our pasts, ethnicities, traditions, or religious backgrounds), and our view of one another (as people who are all part of the Body of Christ, who are united as one).

And the gospel is still challenging us to do the same thing today.

It certainly did for me.

Encountering Christ helped me restore my view of my heavenly father (which had been tarnished by my alcoholic, angry, abusive earthly father), my view of myself (which was riddled with insecurities that stemmed from the trauma I'd experienced with my dad), and my view of my earthly father (which was plagued by bitterness and judgment).

My friend recently asked me a philosophical question, "Who are you?"

I thought about his question then answered, "I am a child of God. I'm a husband, father, and son; I'm a producer, podcast host, blogger, editor, and social media strategist; I'm a Celtics, Mets, and Cowboys fan, a sports nut. But when you strip down all the labels, at the core of who I am is Christ in me (Colossians 1:27), someone who is loved by God."

> *"Encountering Christ helped me restore my view of my heavenly father (which had been tarnished by my alcoholic, angry, abusive earthly father), my view of myself (which was riddled with insecurities that stemmed from the trauma I'd experienced with my dad), and my view of my earthly father (which was plagued by bitterness and judgment)."*

My friend then asked me, "Who is your dad?"

I again thought about his question then answered, "My dad is a child of God, too. He's a grandfather, father, and son; he's a Celtics, Cardinals, and Giants fan, a sports nut. And again, when you strip down all the labels, at the core of who he is, is someone who is loved by God."

What was interesting to me about the conversation was my realization that my dad and I were exactly the same at a core level. Just like my brother Chris had told me, the Cross of Jesus Christ created a level playing field for all of us.

There is a verse in the Bible that has always reminded me of my father: Romans 7:15. In the verse, Paul transparently shares his struggles with his own humanity. He says, "I do not understand what I do. For what I want to do I do not do, but what I hate I do."

When I first read that verse, I thought to myself, *That is Joe Romano to a T.* He truly hated the fact that he drank and the horrible repercussions of his drinking—especially how he hurt those he loved the most. But now I can see that Romans 7:15 describes me as well. I fought with bitterness as Joe battled alcoholism.

It took a long time for me to grasp that my dad was loved by God, because Dad hurt the people who deeply loved him. Sometimes I honestly didn't like believing that he was loved by God because I wanted to hate him. I didn't like believing that he was a child of God because I wanted to make him my enemy. It felt unfair—until I realized that I also mess up and need to be shown mercy and forgiveness.

My dad and I are both deeply loved.

We are both in deep need of radical saving grace.

We both have our own struggles, our own crosses to bear.

We are the *same* person at our cores.

PART V
RECONCILIATION

"The world is overcome not through destruction, but through reconciliation. Not ideals, nor programs, nor conscience, nor duty, nor responsibility, nor virtue, but only God's perfect love can encounter reality and overcome it. Nor is it some universal idea of love, but rather the love of God in Jesus Christ, a love genuinely lived, that does this."

Dietrich Bonhoeffer, *Meditations on the Cross*

21
A Night at the Garden

We have reached the end of this book. Part V, "Reconciliation," is not mentioned in my note to the reader or the table of contents because I didn't want to give away the ending. It is also only one chapter long because my reconciliation with my dad is a story that is still being written.

Our relationship is still healing.

It still has a long way to go.

We have not arrived.

In his article "Serving Each Other Through Forgiveness and Reconciliation" on thrivingpastor.com, Timothy Keller writes,

> *Forgiveness means a willingness to try to reestablish trust, but that reestablishment is always a process. The speed and degree of this restoration entail the re-creation of trust, and that takes time, depending on the nature and severity of the offenses involved. Until a person shows evidence of true change, we should not trust him or her. To immediately give one's trust to a person with sinful habits could actually be enabling him to sin. Trust must be restored, and the speed at which this occurs depends on the behavior.*

My relationship with my dad might always be healing—always moving deeper into reconciliation—because of the unfathomable amount of pain there, some that is still unprocessed on both of our ends. But at the same time, it's also important to note that our relationship is better than it has ever been.

In this chapter, I want to briefly recap my journey with my dad and highlight an area in our relationship that has always been a safe place for us for us to come together throughout his journey fighting alcoholism and mine fighting bitterness. It is a reflection of the reconciliation we've always craved.

But it wasn't until I allowed myself to fully feel my pain, evaluate it, transform it, and forgive the person who caused it that reconciliation became a reality.

∞

The nineties were a dark and lost time for my dad because of his alcoholism; he was in and out of rehab facilities the entire decade.

In the nineties, he missed my high school graduation, his phone calls began, he made up the story about our stepmom dying, he got his first DWI, he first mentioned the word "suicide," he missed my college graduation, and he missed my wedding.

On March 4, 1994, however—a date I remember specifically because it was the day that actor John Candy tragically had a heart attack and died—my father and I had a rare moment of reconciliation when I drove us to Beantown to watch the Celtics play the Lakers at the Boston Garden. It was our first time (in-person, together) watching our favorite basketball team, the Celtics, play during a regular season game. It was a great time. The Celtics won 109-99, but even better than that, Dad didn't drink.

Despite the tension that was steadily building in our relationship during those years, watching the Boston Celtics was always a good way to talk about something that we both enjoyed. Whereas Giants-Cowboys games and Cardinals-Mets games often involved us transmitting our deepest pains and shames onto one another through our sports talk, Celtics games had the opposite effect on our relationship. They were a safe place. Our appreciation for the Celtics was a common ground; it was where we were the same person.

Where we could forget about the pain and the shame.

Where we could forget about the past.

Where we could enter a rare state of oneness.

∞

I wouldn't have thought my dad's alcoholism could get worse than it was in the nineties, but the first thirteen years of the 2000s proved that notion wrong by a landslide.

Once again in and out of rehab facilities in the 2000s, my dad missed the birth of my only child, he called me repeatedly at work during the Giants-Cowboys game, he got his third DWI and went to jail, and he tried to commit suicide.

Although our relationship was tense, however, we once again shared a moment together through sports. In June of 2008, I remember being deeply entrenched in the Celtics-Lakers NBA Finals matchup. I specifically remember watching Game 4 in my Bristol, Connecticut, home, when the Celtics—led by the "Big Three" (Paul Pierce, Ray Allen, and Kevin Garnett)—came back from a 24-point deficit against the Los Angeles Lakers to take a commanding 3-1 lead in the series. It had taken the Celtics twenty-one years to get back to an NBA Finals, and suddenly they were on the doorstep of bringing a title back to Boston.

By the time Game 4 ended that evening, both my wife and my daughter had already been asleep for a while. I was obviously excited after witnessing such a momentous comeback and seeing my team on the brink of an NBA title, and I wanted to share the moment with someone—particularly my dad.

So I decided to call him.

It was an unnatural thing for me to do, because I very rarely called my father. He was always the one who called me. And for the previous two decades I hadn't liked it when he called me, because I never knew which version of him I'd be getting. But nonetheless, I decided to call him.

Though it was only a three- or four-minute call, it was a special moment. We talked and laughed and fed off one another's joy and energy following such a remarkable comeback.

I'm unsure if there's anything about my dad and his life that I've tried to apply to my own life, but one thing he *did* pass down to me is his love for sports, and even more his love for the Boston Celtics. And there we were—his team, my team, our team—on the brink of winning an NBA title (they ended up winning the series 4-2).

"Good night, Dad," I eventually said. "I hope *we* win it all."

∾

Eight years later, in December of 2016, two days before Dad's birthday, Dad and I returned to Boston to watch a Celtics game together… for the first time in twenty-three years.

The fact that the game took place near his birthday was especially neat because I had never really done anything to celebrate the day he was born. I guess subconsciously my brothers and I were against celebrating the life of someone who had caused some of our deepest wounds. This wasn't fair to Dad, but it's how we felt. All he ever wanted was to be loved, to be understood.

Honestly, it can still be difficult for me to hang out with my dad because of my past scars, but I am getting there. I am in the process of forgiving, just as he is in the process of fighting alcohol. Just as a healing alcoholic hopefully isn't ever ignorant or arrogant enough to believe that he or she has overcome the disease and is no longer an alcoholic, I have accepted that I will always be on the journey of forgiving again and again for the direct and indirect ways I've been hurt and will be hurt. Each day is an opportunity to move toward reconciliation. And *choosing* forgiveness has brought an indescribable freedom to my life the last four years. I am no longer worried about my dad messing up. I am venturing deeper into peace—into truly letting go. This has made me a less anxious husband. A more present father. A more loving person. The burdens I have always carried no longer chain me down.

Anyway, in 2016, my relationship with my dad was in a different state than it had been for most of my life. And if there was one thing that Dad would want for his birthday, it'd be to go to a Celtics game.

All these positive dynamics at play in my own life and in my relationship with my dad made being at the TD Garden together, watching the Celtics (a team that would go on to finish first in the Eastern Conference that year), an even sweeter time. So much had changed since the last time we'd gone to a game together. I had gotten married, found my faith, had a daughter, gotten my dream job at ESPN, and chosen to forgive my dad. He had become a grandfather, gotten sober, and was experiencing a joy and normalcy in life he hadn't experienced in decades.

At one point during the game, Dad rose from his seat and told me that he was going to get a soda from the concession stand. I was reminded of how, just a few years before, I would have been concerned—downright scared—that he would return to the game hammered and would humiliate himself and me through his angry, out-of-control yelling.

But this time, I wasn't really concerned at all. Those days are long gone.

Later during the game, I had some big news I wanted to share with him, something that I had known for a few weeks: my ESPN career was coming to an end. After almost seventeen years of working there, I'd felt the call to do more for God and to use my talents, my skills, and my experiences in a new way. I had to tell my dad—the most sports-obsessed man I knew—that his son was going to no longer be working for The Worldwide Leader in Sports.

I was a little nervous to share my latest career move with him because, knowing his love for sports, I think he took a lot of pride in telling people that his son worked for the biggest sports media company there is. But to my surprise, my dad didn't ridicule my decision or my desires. He didn't even question them. He told me that I should do whatever I thought was best and whatever made me happy. That meant a lot to me.

I also told him about this book—how I hoped that our broken story could continue to turn into something beautiful on a personal level and how perhaps our broken relationship—the struggles, the pain, all of it—could truly help others. To inspire people to forgive. To inspire people to make good decisions. To help people move toward peace and healing. Dad gave me his blessing to write it.

It's sometimes difficult to get my dad to talk about deep things and to be fully transparent—maybe because of the physical effect that his decades of bingeing has had on his brain or maybe because he thinks I'm judging him (because I judged him for so many years)—but our conversation at the Garden was the most transparent, vulnerable conversation I'd ever had with him.

I've noticed that there have been a lot of starts—fresh beginnings—in the different aspects of my relationship with my dad since I decided to *truly* forgive him without conditions.

∞

On the other side of forgiveness, there is a possibility for love and restoration.

There isn't always restoration on the other side of forgiveness, but forgiveness at least gives restoration a chance to unfold as boundaries create time for us to heal.

I still have triggers, directly and indirectly. I still have wounds from my past. I still have emotional and mental feedback cycles in my relationship with my dad that I need to explore. But whenever something arises within me, as unexpected as it might be, I believe it is actually a gateway into introspection: into feeling, evaluating, transforming, and ultimately forgiving—and then forgiving again and again.

I know how hard this is for many of you who are reading. Broken relationships are not always restored. But I want to encourage you: nothing is ever hopeless. Forgiveness is always possible. Healing is always possible. Though a relationship might not ever be fully healed, *you* can be fully healed through your willingness to feel, evaluate, transform, and surrender the pain.

Sitting there at the Garden next to my father in December, as strange as this might sound, I felt like *I* was the proud dad seeing his son on the other side of something he'd fought for years. I'd seen my dad emerge from the dark night of the soul—a despair that had almost claimed him for good. I'd seen him take intentional steps toward sobriety and getting his life back in order. I was so very proud.

My dad's battle with alcoholism has taught me many things *not* to do in life. But one thing it has taught me *to* do is to fight. To fight the demons inside. To fight for those you love. To fight for what you believe in. In fact, that might be the best word to describe my father: fighter. That's who Joe Romano is. He is a fighter. He taught me to never, ever give up.

I'm again reminded of *Star Wars*—this time *Return of the Jedi*. In this chapter of the saga, we witness Darth Vader's fighting spirit. Though he has done some horrible things in the galaxy, he never gives up on—nor fully betrays—the goodness that is deep within him. At the end of the movie, when Luke Skywalker is being electrocuted by The Emperor and is on the doorstep of death, we witness the fullness of Vader's fighting spirit. Vader, overcome with emotion by the pain his son is in, unexpectedly picks up The Emperor and throws him off a platform to his death. Vader physically saves Luke. Luke psychologically—and emotionally and maybe spiritually—saves Vader.

My dad fought and fought and fought, and instead of allowing himself to succumb to the alcoholism or depression or anxiety, he always confronted it head-on. When he was in and out of rehab facilities, I sometimes felt like his life had become a broken record. Addiction is a serious thing, however, and what was *really* unfolding was a courageous fight—a beautiful life of never giving up.

"Though a relationship might not ever be fully healed, you can be fully healed through your willingness to feel, evaluate, transform, and surrender the pain."

I look up to my dad for how he has fought through four decades of hell. And his ability and willingness to fight have led to moments like the one we shared at the Boston Celtics game that night at the Garden—moments that feel an awful lot like heaven.

At one point in the second half, I turned to Joe Romano—*my father*—and said to him, "I'm proud of you, Dad."

And I always will be.

Because he taught me to fight.

To fight bitterness.

To fight the temptation to lose hope.

To fight for our loved ones—through learning more and more about grace and the beautiful struggle to forgive.

Jason and Joe Romano at the TD Garden in Boston, Massachusetts, on December 16, 2016.

Acknowledgments

First, I wanted to thank YOU, the reader, for taking the time to invest in this book and experience the power of forgiveness.

Thank you, Dawn, for believing in me and allowing me to take on a book project when it made no sense to do such a thing. You are my rock momma, and I love you!

Thank you to my daughter, Sarah. My miracle child. God's most precious gift to me. I love you more than you'll ever know and am so proud of the young lady you are becoming.

Thank you to Chris and Damian. My two best friends and the greatest brothers a person could ever ask for. This book isn't just my journey—this is our journey, and I'm grateful to share life with both of you. Romano brothers forever!

Thank you, Mom. When Dad wasn't there, you were. And you've always been. You've kept our family in tact and have been the heart and soul of all that we have accomplished. I love you!

Thank you, The Core Media Group and Robert Walker, for believing in this project from the very first phone call.

Thank you, Stephen Copeland, for being an amazing partner in putting this book together. You are a gifted writer and collaborator, but even more, an awesome friend.

Thank you to Pastor Joe, and my Hillside Community Church family for pouring into me and my family this last decade. May the name of Jesus continue to be lifted high in Bristol, Connecticut.

Thank you, Caleb Kaltenbach. In early 2016, you were the first person to suggest I write a book and tell my story of forgiveness. I'm grateful for you and your friendship.

Thank you to Brandon Marshall, Jon Gordon, Alan Major, Bomani

Jones, Lorenzo Alexander, London Fletcher, Alejandro Reyes, Danny Kanell, Ryan Clark, Sam Acho, Adam Richman, and so many others whose generous support helped make this book a reality. You'll never know how much your kindness has meant to me.

Thank you, Scott Black, for your friendship. Every time we go to breakfast, I learn something from you. You are an amazing example of what it looks like to be a husband and father. Love you, bro. Go Cowboys!

Thank you to Darryl Strawberry. At ten years old, you helped me fall in love with baseball. You were my childhood sports hero. Now, many years later, you've helped me once again by showing me that God is truly in the restoration business. I'm forever grateful for your willingness to be a part of this book.

Lastly, thank you to Joe Romano, my father. Dad, you've been through hell and back. We've had the highest of highs and the lowest of lows. And through it all, you have always fought back. Even when you wanted to give up, you didn't. Thank you for being willing to share our story and allowing the good, the bad, the pain, the hurt, the anger, and the love to all be spread out into this book. I love you and am thankful you're my dad.

To God be the glory.